Managing Change in Higher Education: Preparing for the 21st Century

Edited by:

K. Scott Hughes
Principal
KPMG Peat Marwick

Daryl Conner
President
ODR, Inc.

College and University Personnel Association

Table of Contents

Preface ix
   Daryl R. Conner

1. How Disruptions or Changes
   Affect Our Behavior 1
   Frederick Turk

2. Viewing Change as a Way of Life 15
   Ruzwa Cooper

3. Examining the Roles of
   Those Affected by Change 25
   Alceste Pappas

4. The Role and Responsibility
   of the Sponsor 35
   Brian Gorman

5. Understanding that Resistance
   to Change is Inevitable 53
   Warren Riley

6. Organizational Culture and Change 67
   Barbara Horst

7. Taking a Structured and Disciplined
   Approach to Managing Change 79
   K. Scott Hughes

The College and University Personnel Association (CUPA) is an international network of more than 4,500 personnel administrators representing more than 1,400 colleges and universities. Through regular and special publications and studies, CUPA works to keep its members informed of the latest legal, legislative, and regulatory developments affecting personnel administration, as well as trends and innovative policies and practices in the field. Services include a semimonthly newsletter, a journal, an annual convention, regional meetings, and seminars on timely topics of special interest to the personnel profession. For further information, on books of related interest, or for a catalog of CUPA publications, contact, CUPA, 1233 Twentieth St., N.W., Suite 503, Washington DC, 20036, (202) 429-0311.

Copyright © 1989 by the College and University
Personnel Association
1233 20th St., N.W., Suite 503
Washington, DC, 20036
All rights reserved
Printed in the United States of America

Cover design by Pamela Wells
ISBN: 0-910402-92-2

CUPA Publications and Research Advisory Board

Daniel J. Julius, *Vice President for Publications and Research, CUPA*
    Associate Vice President for Academic Affairs
    University of San Francisco

Judith Anderson, Director of Affirmative Action
    Eastern Illinois University

C. Keith Groty, Assistant Vice President for
    Personnel and Employee Relations
    Michigan State University

Joanel Zeller Huart, Senior Human Resource Analyst
    Washington Higher Education Personnel Board

Edward J. Kelley, Assistant to the President
    State University of New York, College at Brockport

Barbara Nicholson-Brown, Associate Director, Personnel Services
    St. Mary's College of California

Frank J. Skahill, Vice President for Human Relations
    Community College of Philadelphia

Anita Webb-Lupo, Assistant Provost/Professor
    Illinois State University

Acknowledgments

This monograph is the composite work of several individuals dedicated to the value and belief systems of higher education in this nation. They work as advisors to governing boards, presidents, chancellors and chief financial officers of academic institutions, ranging from the very large statewide systems to the very small private liberal arts colleges.

The co-editors of the monograph are Daryl R. Conner and K. Scott Hughes. Daryl R. Conner is president of ODR, Inc., an Atlanta-based training and consulting firm. K. Scott Hughes is a principal with KPMG Peat Marwick and directs its western region management consulting practice for educational institutions.

The authors are members of the KPMG Peat Marwick Higher Education Management Consulting Group. They focus on helping colleges and universities change and respond to the dynamic forces that impact their programs and services.

Special recognition is due to Warren Smith, director of communications of ODR, who provided valuable assistance in developing the ODR concepts to the higher education culture. Finally, special thanks to Evangeline Tolleson, who applied her professional editorial expertise to the manuscript.

Preface

This monograph describes a structured methodology to implement organizational change within higher education. The Managing Organizational Change (MOC) methodology results from more than 15 years of observing and analyzing literally thousands of client engagements with organizations large and small—including Fortune 500 corporations, non-profits and such governmental bodies as the U.S. Congress and the White House staff.

Due to the growing influence of multinational corporations and the global nature of many economic, political and environmental crises, MOC is now applied by business and political leaders throughout Europe, the Soviet Union, Latin America and Asia. The concepts in this book are especially suited for higher education institutions because of their origins and philosophy.

First, the origins. In 1970, a career in organizational development—behavioral science applied to an organizational setting—was probably the last thing on my mind. Completing a graduate degree in "humanistic psychology" at West Georgia College, I was well on my way to a career as a clinician and had never even heard of organizational development. But the college was planning a major reorganization, and the head of the psychology department submitted my name for an assistantship to consult on the human aspects of the change effort. I decided to accept the assistantship, and my first organizational development assignment had begun.

My academic training and clinical experience—in the U.S. Army and at the local mental health clinic—gave me just enough naive confidence to think I had a sufficient background to understand the dynamics of change as they occur on the personal level. I believed that clinical psychology was simply a matter of helping *people* develop tools to cope with change, so why wouldn't my training work with *organizations* as well? Fortunately, my arrogance had limits—at least I knew that I did not fully comprehend how all individuals would respond to organizational change.

So, in typical graduate student fashion, my first stop was to the library. And, as luck would have it, I found two books that—unknown to me then—are classics in the field: *The Dynamics of Change* by Warren Bennis (and others) and *Process Consultation* by Edgar Schein. These books helped me see that an organizational consultant and a therapist are very similar. Both see many of the same pathologies, but deal with quite different manifestations. They must understand many similar principles and master the same techniques to empower their clients to overcome problems or take advantage of opportunities.

Principles of Higher Education

How MOC methodology applies to higher education results from much more than its origins by chance in a college setting. Much of MOC's underpinnings and philosophy comes from the same principles that form the justification for higher education.

First, the entire education process is based upon change. At its most basic and personal level, the mission of education—primary, secondary and higher—is nothing less than the individual's transformation. This has profound social implications: Education changes the individual, and the educated individual changes the society where he (or she) resides.

History provides us with untold numbers of examples where education led the way in the birth and rebirth of nations. Thomas

Jefferson viewed the pinnacle of his career not during his tenure as president of the United States, but as president of the University of Virginia. After the Civil War, Robert E. Lee shunned all political activity in favor of fulfilling his duties as president of Washington (later Washington & Lee) College. Both men understood that fundamental changes in a nation or a culture could not occur without an infrastructure of education in place.

Historically, higher education institutions have been places to study subtle, mysterious phenomena. Next they became the repositories for the wisdom gained from these studies. Finally, they are places that educate others about these phenomena. In many ways, my firm—ODR, Inc.—operates with much the same agenda as a "university of change." The knowledge I gained from my first assignment at West Georgia College nearly 20 years ago has been supplemented with data from more than 1,000 organizations. ODR's early research was qualitative and very similar to what social scientists call "field research." ODR consultants served as participants/observers—both students and participants of change management. After a consultation they would record their observations and tentative conclusions, compile them into diagnostic instruments or principles, and eventually develop a complete methodology. This process, in fact, continues as we take constantly updated versions of the methodology to yet more clients.

Now more than 30 tools or aids are embedded in the MOC methodology. The tools include instruments that evaluate commitment to change, identify the anticipated level of resistance, assess the strength of the team responsible for managing the change, and examine the current organization's stress level.

Over time we began to encounter people who wanted, in a sense, "to join the faculty" by developing their understanding of the MOC methodology so that they could apply it to a broad range of organizations. In exchange, they would help us in our continuing efforts to refine the methodology. ODR works regularly with organizations such as KPMG Peat Marwick, which developed expertise in MOC to implement change within their existing and newly formed client relationships. ODR's "strategic alliance" with Peat Marwick has resulted in training of their consultants worldwide. The authors of the following chapters are, in fact, some of those consultants who are experts on specific issues related to higher education institutions. As a result of training from ODR, they possess a sophisticated understanding of change management. Each of the seven chapters in this monograph represent the principles developed by ODR and applied by these KPMG consultants in a higher education environment.

This book's structure and contents could serve as a metaphor for ODR's commitment to transfer the methodology to those who can make a difference in the world. This book was written by men and women who are accessible to the leaders of colleges and universities, and possess a single-minded commitment to higher education institutions. Their capacity to truly "make a difference" in this setting is far greater than mine alone.

The true key to reform is continual self-renewal. The MOC methodology is based on the belief that change is a process we continually experience. MOC is not merely an instrument to implement a computer system or reorganize a departmental structure, though it often is used for these projects. Problems associated with higher education do not yield to a simple monolithic response. The answer to the crises facing higher education lies not in new computer systems, accountability, business techniques, curriculum "relevancy" or other single-issue solutions.

Having a tool to help implement occasional change or even a system that drives dramatic change is not enough. The *culture* of higher education must be developed to accommodate and even initiate constant change. Somehow, the stability required for thoughtful research and education must exist within an increasingly dynamic environment. This stability is built not by slowing down the environment, but by increasing one's capacity to assimilate change. MOC is designed to do just that.

Change: A Constant Process

While setting me on a new career course, the West Georgia College organizational development assignment taught me basic principles and gave me an experiential understanding that change is constant. I also developed an abiding interest in contributing to the informed management of colleges and universities. My conclusion is that higher education institutions need a vision that transcends immediate political, economic and logistic circumstances on the one hand and social activism on the other. This does not mean that these realities should be ignored. Rather, the institution should be self-renewing both physically and philosophically. It should exist for a reason that supercedes historical moments in time, and it should develop a continually adjusted process for dealing with emerging opportunities and challenges.

Finally, and perhaps most importantly, higher education is about empowerment. The only worthwhile education is one that provides a way for people "to learn how to learn." The changes that education bring are not merely from one static and discreet state to another: The process of growth and change becomes continual. Our philosophy of transferring the methodology—giving people and organizations not just a tool for a specific change, but a way to process continual change—is perhaps our strongest link to higher education institutions.

I sincerely hope that the following principles of the Managing Organizational Change methodology can help colleges and universities create a self-renewal process that is so desperately needed today nationwide and throughout the world.

Daryl R. Conner
October 1989

1
How Disruptions or Changes Affect Our Behavior

By Frederick Turk

A quick look through the *Chronicle of Higher Education, Change* magazine and other higher education journals reveals even to the casual observer that college and university leaders face an increasingly complex environment. Adaptation to new technologies, the doubling of information every two years, and the need to replace an aging faculty are among the major fundamental issues facing leaders in higher education. As these and other factors influencing our environment increase in number and complexity, the ability to adapt to these changes becomes more difficult. Much that Alvin Toffler predicted in his book *Future Shock*—written in the late 1960s regarding human inability to respond to rapid change—has become reality in the 1980s.

Change is more rapid than ever in our academic settings. Fundamental changes are affecting the economic, political, psychological, sociological, theological, technological and organizational underpinnings of our institutions. We must observe, plan and act to recognize change and master the dangers and opportunities facing our colleges and universities.

Changing Higher Education

The changes that academic institutions must endure while adapting to today's environment are beyond precise calculation. The pace of change is increasing and its forces are pressing organizations from all directions. Higher education institutions as centers of learning, research and public service—face changes that significantly influence the scope, structure and function of their activities.

Colleges and universities are experiencing a *complexity explosion* that is accelerating. The issues embedded here come from two dimensions: *Macro changes* which are external to the institution and fundamentally change its future behavior; and *micro changes* which are internal and affect the institution's ability to respond to external changes.

Macro changes relate to fundamental factors, such as an increasingly diverse population that creates major social and educational problems. For example:

- More than 25 million people in the United States are functionally illiterate, and high school dropout rates remain especially high in urban areas.
- One-third of our population will consist of minorities by 1995.
- The aging of our population creates a larger group of elderly people who live longer, are more energetic and seek a continued educational experience.
- Our changing work environment demands more flexible and better educated employees who can cope with changing job requirements.

The United States faces a crisis of managing finite resources with infinite demands as we approach the 21st century. Our nation's budget deficits in the 1980s are a pressing issue that the administration and Congress must resolve. Federal support to colleges has stabilized and continuing pressure will be exerted to reduce government support for financial aid, research and other important programs—even though such investments in people and knowledge are essential for making us a strong and vibrant nation in the next century. Competition increases for limited private dollars that help meet our expanding educational needs. Finally, the ability of students, parents and corporations to pay for education and research services is diminishing. As taxpayers and consumers for higher education, we are becoming increasingly vocal and reticent to accept the rising cost of education.

The macro changes present a difficult dilemma for colleges and universities. On the one hand, we hear increasing demands to be opportunistic and fulfill a role that can lead the nation into the 21st century, solving many serious ills of our society. On the other hand, we also face a serious lack of resources to do the job. Institutions that can solve this dilemma will likely be the very successful ones.

Colleges and universities also face many *micro changes*. Our institutions must strengthen programs to attract and retain quality faculty—a special challenge considering that 25 percent of faculty will be eligible to retire by 1995 without replacements ready to fill the void. In some disciplines, there are already insufficient Ph.D.s to meet future needs. Many institutions also must expand and improve facilities to meet the needs of future generations, and face major investments to support infrastructure and costly new technology for instruction and research. These changes substantially impact how educational programs are conducted, and how faculty teach and students learn. Colleges and universities must address these issues to respond effectively to the market demands of students, faculty, alumni, government, the private sector and others.

Our institutions are experiencing a number of organizational changes that will address these pressures. Typical examples are:

- *Leadership change* – responding to needs for new presidential and governing board expertise that brings a new institutional vision.

- *Reorganization* – restructuring organizations and human resources to cope with continual changes and take advantage of opportunities.
- *Technology* – adapting to rapidly changing technology in the delivery of academic programs by the faculty, and transforming the behavior of all users.
- *Modifying programs* – focusing on strengths and introducing curricula changes, new faculty and new workload expectations.
- *Constituency development* – changing the approach and attitude of faculty, administration and staff regarding their responsibility to build support among students, alumni, friends, government and the private sector.

The changes cited above fundamentally impact everyone associated with a college or university. Our ability to cope with these changes will determine our ultimate success.

How Change Causes Disruption

Change would be relatively simple if limited to items. Changes of any type, however, also affect people and their behaviors. Managers who successfully implement change must consider the human aspect.

When we introduce change within our institutions, we often understand little about influencing human behavior. Nor do we understand the dynamics of change, the natural human resistance or processes for gaining cooperation.

Before delving into processes to achieve change—to be covered in later chapters—we should first understand how change causes disruption. To function in a world constantly in flux, most people deal with the discomfort of uncertainty by trying to maintain control over their lives. People feel a sense of control when they understand their environment and can adapt to change as it occurs.

This understanding derives from a person's mind set or *frame of reference* concerning life. A frame of reference is based on a perception of reality and dictates how a person selects what to perceive and how to interpret it. A frame of reference allows someone to understand what happens in his (or her) life and what to expect in the future. By predicting and planning the future, the individual reduces feelings of uncertainty and achieves a sense of control. The accompanying illustration on frame of reference shows how we comprehend our reality and respond to experiences.

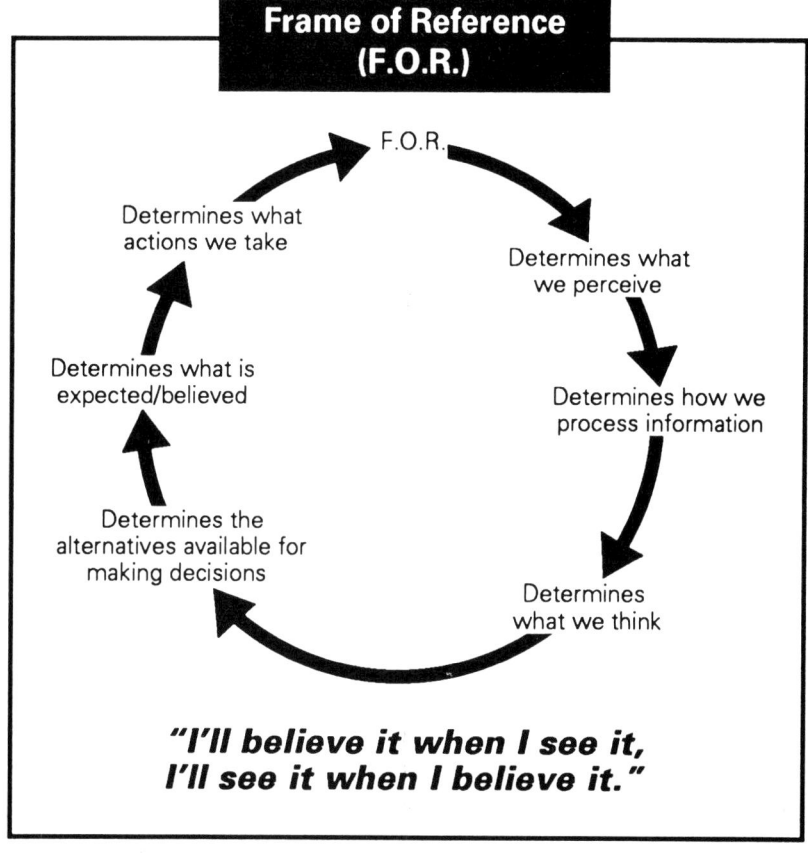

©1989 by ODR, Inc., *Managing Organizational Change: Implementation Planning Procedure.*

The ability to develop an accurate prediction of one's future can reduce uncertainty. Disrupting an individual's expectation pattern causes one of two basic psychological reactions:

- ***Minor change*** does not significantly threaten expectations, but causes the individual to make adjustments to restructure expectations and adapt to change. These common adjustments typically go unnoticed, leaving the impression that change hasn't even occurred.
- ***Major change*** causes old expectations to become invalid, motivating such reactions as uncertainty, fear, disorientation, confusion and loss of equilibrium. These feelings result from inconsistencies between what was expected and what is perceived. When change disrupts a person's frame of reference, he no longer knows what to expect from himself or others. The resulting stress can generate disabling consequences for an individual and cause costly lost production and benefit to their organizations.

Crisis results from a breakdown in the established relationship between an individual and his expectations of the environment. Whether planned or unplanned, voluntary or involuntary, major changes that disrupt expectations always cause a certain level of crisis. With this general framework, we can examine how these dynamics affect an individual in a changing organization.

How People React to Change

When crisis due to major change develops in an organization, people respond in one of two different ways:

Type D Response (Danger oriented reaction to change)

People in this group are unprepared for the ambiguity that results from change, and may feel uncertain about themselves and others. They do not understand the dynamics of change and feel a need for self defense.

Individuals in this group use a variety of mechanisms to reinforce their own frame of reference regarding change. These defense mechanisms include:
- Denial of change or its impact. *("We don't need a new enrollment management program.")*
- Consciously or unconsciously disorienting information related to the change. *("Well, student enrollment levels aren't that bad.")*
- Acknowledging the change but relieving the anxiety by convincing themselves and others it won't really affect the status quo. *("This new enrollment management program is just a new name for our traditional and proven admission program.")*

Type D people faced with organizational change respond reactively rather than proactively, and deny the forces of change for as long as possible. Their behavior can be hostile, argumentative, defensive, angry and depressive. They are not prepared for the insecure feelings created by the disruption to their personal work environment. When they can no longer ignore a major change, they don't have enough time to plan an appropriate response strategy. The need to change is invariably acknowledged late, so they feel justified in their "knee-jerk" reactions. Such last-minute reactions to change are typically ineffective in the fast-paced environment of most modern organizations. Even more disturbing, these people would be no more effective if they took time to plan as they should. They simply lack conceptual tools and interpersonal skills to diagnose the need for change, design an action plan and implement it.

In the past, the rate and speed of organizational change in our academic institutions was slow enough to accommodate people with Type D personalities. The pace of major change was evolutionary; disruptive impact was easier to avoid, and individuals simply had more time to adapt to the changes. In today's turbulent environment, with high demand for advanced educational services and limited resources, these people are experiencing gaping holes in their defenses against change. As the reality of change pours in, they feel overwhelmed and incapable in a world they perceive as unpredictable, confusing and contradictory.

The Type D response is not limited to older people or the "soon to retire." Because the need to train people in change-related strategies and tactics is not recognized by most colleges, graduate schools or management training programs, many young people demonstrate definite Type D characteristics. Type D response to the crisis of change is affected by one's need for security; stress tolerance; use of defense mechanisms; tolerance for ambiguity; creativity level; problem-solving abilities; past experiences with major change; ability to generate new frames of reference; and training in how to respond to organizational crisis.

Type O (Opportunity oriented reaction to change)

Type O people respond to the crisis of change much differently. This group feels as disoriented as Type D people when disruption occurs, but experiences less need to defend against such feelings. Disruption and the accompanying discomforts are viewed as a necessary (though unpleasant) part of the adjustment process that all people experience when adapting to a major change. Type O people feel sensitive to the needs of others during important organizational changes because they understand and accept the psychological processes that occur when a work environment is altered. Their sensitivity to personal and technical aspects of a changing organization helps them plan and implement changes with minimum resistance and maximum support. This ability becomes a major advantage in responding to necessary organizational changes.

In colleges and universities, Type O people are those who relish the new organizational structure or computer system. They see opportunities for advancement and a time to exercise their creative juices. Frequently singled out to lead change efforts, they are the ones who rise above their colleagues.

Another important characteristic of Type O people is their

acceptance of change as a natural part of living. *Future Shock* is the degree of disorientation we experience when encountering new realities that are dramatically different from our old operating expectations. Type D people develop expectations void of major change, and therefore suffer tremendous shock when established realities suddenly shift. The Type O group feels less intensity because change does not shatter their expectations. They did not anticipate their world would remain unchanged. Change, even when it is major or unanticipated, is viewed as part of organizational life—a challenge to conquer or a problem to solve, not a dilemma to avoid.

The Type O's ability to respond positively to change does not occur because of any special immunity to the stress of change. When faced with disruptive change, they are as vulnerable to confusion and anxiety as Type D people. Understanding human behavior does not mean one does not feel the impact of change or can circumvent its unpleasant parts. Love, pain, frustration and joy are experienced by all people, regardless of whether they understand the psychological dynamics. The same certainly is true for feelings in the crisis of change. The important difference between the two groups is not their reaction to the change, but their reaction to the feelings ignited by change. Type Ds tend to become immobilized by fear, denial or complacency. Type Os recognize their discomfort as a signal to activate their coping mechanisms and adapt to the change—thus generating new *opportunities*.

Outcomes: Type D, Type O

To avoid their fear of change or lack of knowledge about what to do, Type D people often react to disruption by throwing up a smoke screen and blaming someone or something for the problems caused by change. *"If only Jones had corrected the course scheduling program, we wouldn't be in this student registration mess."* This behavior is both demoralizing and counterproductive; blaming and attacking only result in counterattacks.

In contrast, to mobilize their coping mechanisms, Type O

people shift to a problem-solving position. Instead of blaming others, they return to the beginning of the process and incorporate what they have learned from the change into a new understanding of the situation, or they develop a new frame of reference. This process of updating relevant information helps them see the situation differently. The impact of change no longer clashes with their new understanding of reality. By modifying their frame of reference, they alter their expectations and come up with creative new approaches to the problem. As they create solutions, they become more stable and productive. Only a matter of time exists until more change disrupts and alters expectations, and the Type O person begins the process again *(see Figure 1)*.

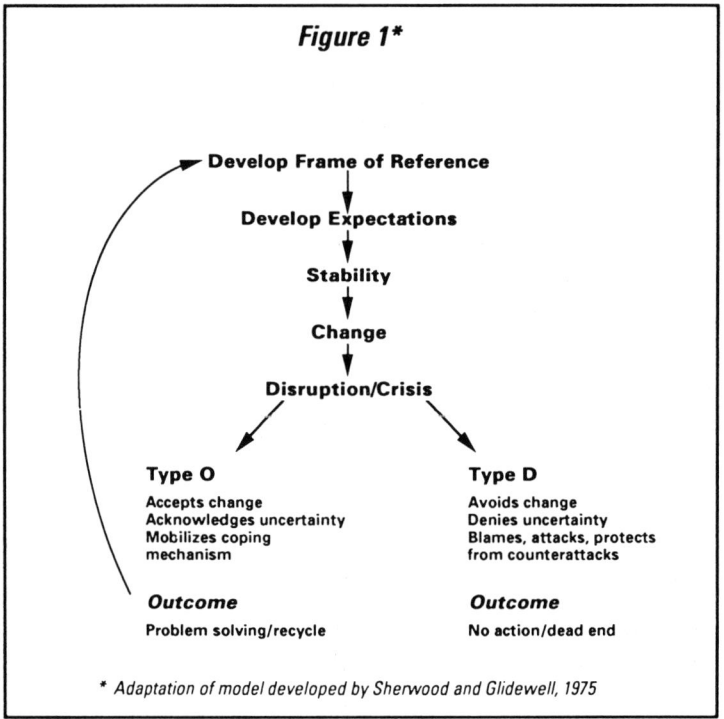

© 1989 by ODR, Inc., *Managing Organizational Change: Dangers & Opportunities.*

By approaching change in this way, Type Os demonstrate an aspect of the Chinese philosophy of crisis. In fact, the Chinese represent the "crisis of change" not with one character, but two *(see illustration)*. The upper character represents "danger," while the lower one conveys "hidden opportunity."

Change is continual and always will be a key variable in organizational survival. To remain viable leaders in our turbulent environment, organizational managers need the skills to cope with change. Organizational change cannot be avoided, circumvented or camouflaged away as a Type D person attempts to do. If the manager understands the dynamics of change and manages the process repeatedly, new opportunities will emerge. Ignored or mismanaged consequences, on the other hand, can be very dangerous.

Type O Skills Can Be Learned

For colleges and universities to survive, prosper and meet the challenges of the next century, academic leaders, faculty and managers must obtain the knowledge and skills to design and implement successful strategies for coping with the pressures of change. This is not a call for training more change "experts" housed in "change departments" within organizations. Having access to internal specialists or external consultants trained in facilitating organizational change is a critical part of a system's plan for change project. However, relying solely on experts causes problems because this approach isolates the change specialists.

All management levels should be trained and supervised in the skills of implementing organizational change. These change agents do not need to be experts in the change field but should use Type O skills as they diagnose needs for change and design strategies to implement changes with minimum resistance and maximum support. Specifically, change agents need knowledge and skills in the following areas:

- How to manage change effectively.
- How people change, and how they resist change.
- How to diagnose an organization's readiness for change.
- How to design change plans.
- How to identify and relate to people's emotional responses to change.
- How to reduce and manage negative reactions to change.
- How to effectively communicate change plans.

Our world is changing at an ever-increasing rate. For colleges and universities to sustain themselves, academic leadership must learn to design a path through the turbulence. The forces of change pressuring academic institutions today are extremely complicated and demand a high priority to be understood and handled appropriately. Leaders, faculty and managers must possess the knowledge and skill tools to reduce the dangers and increase opportunities of organizational change.

References

Sherwood, J.J., and Glidewell, J.C., "Planned Renegotiation: A Norm-setting O.D. Intervention," in W.W. Burke (Ed.) *New Technologies in Organization Development*, La Jolla, California: University Associates, 1975.

Memorandum to the 41st President of the United States, American Council on Education, January 1988.

American Potential: The Human Dimension, Business–Higher Education Forum of the American Council on Higher Education, 1988.

2
Viewing Change as a Way of Life

By Ruzwa Cooper

> *God, give us the grace to accept with serenity the things that cannot be changed, courage to change the things which should be changed, and the wisdom to distinguish the one from the other.*
>
> Reinhold Neibuhr

Most of us recognize change as an everyday occurrence that manifests itself in biological, intellectual and physical ways all around us. We commonly expect change to happen to others, whether it is personal or professional, and rarely recognize change within ourselves. We often do not recognize change because the process is typically slow, allowing us to absorb the change without significant disruption.

At the organizational level, our higher education institutions have moved from a period of slow, periodic, evolutionary change to a period of continual, explosive change. Not only is the magnitude of change confronting these institutions possibly greater than at any time in their history, but now the change is constant and overlapping. We no longer have the luxury of reacting to singular events in hopes of deflecting their consequences.

Three States of the Change Process

Most managers think of change as a one-step process: a movement from here to there. Rarely do they sufficiently consider what happens in between "here" and "there." What happens in the "in between," however, significantly influences whether an organization can change successfully.

We must recognize that people go through three states during change: *Present State, Transition State* and *Desired State*. Managing this three-step process requires that we consciously and systematically orchestrate the human and organizational variables to achieve the desired state *(see illustration.)*

The *Present State* is the status quo as defined by established expectation patterns, a condition of equilibrium or stable behavior. This state of equilibrium continues indefinitely unless disrupted by force. The resulting pain creates the incentive to move away from the present state.

Rarely do people or organizations change without feeling or expecting pain. People or organizations who are unwilling to accept change generally do not feel or perceive that the pain is sufficiently severe. A college will not seek an aggressive fund-raising capital campaign unless it suffers—or expects to suffer—enough financially or in its programs to warrant the time, energy and risk associated with the campaign effort.

Pain manifests in many ways. On a personal level, pain can surface as a temporary setback, such as a failure to receive an expected promotion or a disappointing relationship. At an organizational level, pain can mean student enrollment declines, loss of public funding or escalating faculty salaries. Movement from the present state toward the desired state generally requires a disruptive

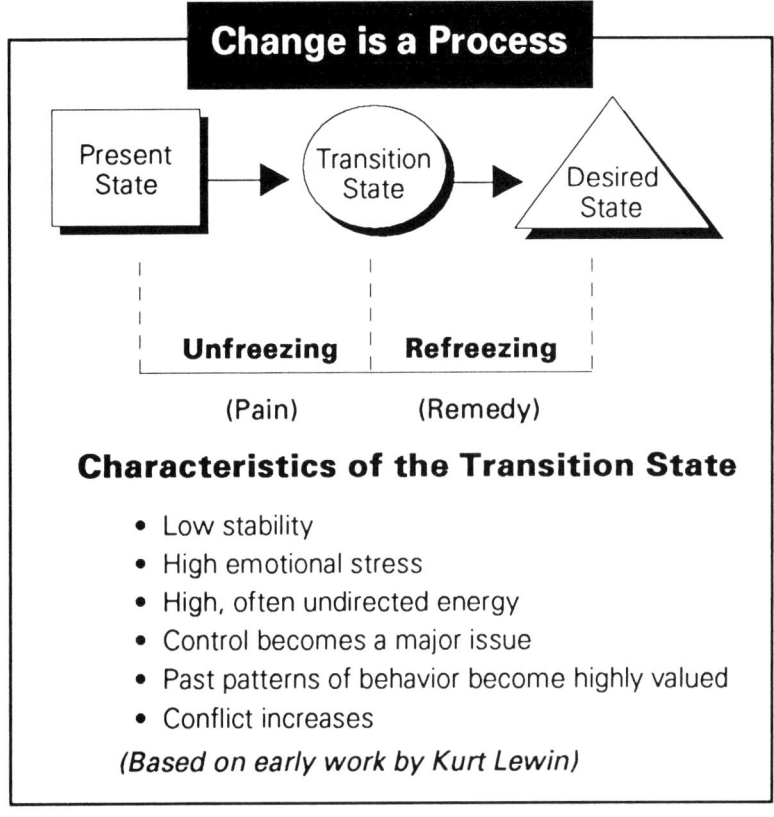

©1989 by ODR, Inc., *Managing Organizational Change: Implementation Planning Procedure.*

force that induces sufficient pain to "unfreeze" the present state. Exploding enrollments in the 1960s, student unrest in the 70s and enrollment declines in the 80s are examples of disruptive forces that have been experienced by higher education institutions.

Transforming an ice cube into a new shape is analogous to the unfreezing process. If this process is not managed correctly, too much heat can be applied and the ice cube will melt and turn into steam. If too little heat is applied, the outside of the cube melts but the core remains solid. Many reorganizations demonstrate this concept well. The organizational chart is clearly changed and reporting lines are shifted, but workers continue to operate along the old, established lines. Change appears to have taken place, but the old methods are as fixed, or frozen, as ever.

The need for a *Transition State* is often ignored or consciously avoided by managers. This is the point where people no longer behave as they did in the past, nor are they fully set in the desired behavior pattern. The equilibrium of the present state has been disrupted and the desired state has not yet been reached.

The transition state is dangerous because it represents disequilibrium. As the Chinese ideogram shown earlier suggests, this also provides a learning opportunity. Those who are asked to change usually are eager to learn ways to reduce the anxieties and stresses associated with the pain of unfreezing. They tend to be open to potential remedies that will alleviate their discomfort.

The transition state, the focal point of the change process, is characterized by ambiguity and insecurity. Previous behavior patterns are no longer acceptable, and desired patterns are not fully learned. The change agent's role is to provide structure to the process by communicating a coherent and consistent vision of the desired state.

An academic institution makes effective use of the transition state with its entering freshmen. The first semester is a powerful form of unfreezing and disrupting old frames of reference. Dormitory living, cafeteria food, new social structures and values, home sickness and loss of close friends leave the new student in a state of confusion or even panic. While these actions disrupt or unfreeze old behavior patterns, they also create an environment for much rapid learning. The resulting tension, caused by the unfreezing, creates the need to operate in new ways that will make sense of the world. The freshman usually learns by Christmas what new behaviors will stabilize the environment and reduce anxiety—perhaps making friends, joining social clubs and studying hard for exams.

The transition state is marked by high ambiguity. People have individual-specific tolerance for ambiguity and will return to the present state during transition unless consequence management is applied. Managing during the transition state involves both high dangers and high opportunities. This unfreezing process invalidates established frames of reference and accepted patterns of behavior, causing people to feel anxious, tense, uncertain, or victims of high emotional stress. Managing this state means managing ambiguity.

Implementing new computer systems are classic examples of a "high danger/high opportunity" transition state. Computer users feel lost, inadequate, frustrated, angry or betrayed as they force themselves to behave differently and adapt to a new computer environment. At the same time, the opportunity is high for increased productivity, improved quality of information and a more user-friendly operating environment.

Managing the transition state also represents high opportunity because the tension caused by unfreezing creates a high need for a new operating framework. The need to reduce anxiety produces a desire for seeking out, processing and utilizing information to create a new stable state. People learn most during the transition state, and a savvy manager can take advantage of this opportunity.

The *Desired State* results from refreezing, stabilizing and integrating the behavior required by the change. It represents the new pattern of expectations and behavior resulting from the change process. The change agent managing this process must provide desirable and accessible alternatives that can serve as the desired state. To implement a new computer system successfully, for example, the users must understand—in their own terms—how the new environment affects them.

Moving Away from the Present State

Two ways of unfreezing the Present State are discussed here—the architectural and hammer approaches. The *architectural approach* to managing the change process requires a thorough implementation plan and may cost much time and energy. Its results often last longer than the hammer approach because it promotes a climate that motivates people to discontinue their previous behavior, thus avoiding high resistance typically associated with force. While costly up front, this approach generally requires little maintenance to ensure continuity and effectiveness. A new computer system, for example, can be implemented with a lengthy plan and much training, or can be substituted overnight with the expectation of high error rates, turnover and general employee dissatisfaction.

The *hammer approach* forces the target population into the desired state as rapidly as possible. This approach helps when immediate results are essential and psychological commitment by the targets of change is not necessary. However, it is often overused and creates high target resistance. Morale problems, lack of drive, apathy and direct sabotage are typical responses to strong-arm techniques.

Both the hammer and architectural methods have associated costs. The hammer approach requires *healing*—one must pay for compliance and in return gets little commitment. The architectural approach requires measures of *prevention* —one must pay the high start-up cost for stronger levels of long-term commitment.

Pain Management

Change occurs when the cost of the status quo is greater than the cost of transition to a new or desired state.

People experience two types of pain. Change-related pain refers to the level of discomfort a person feels when goals are not met (*current pain*) or are not expected to be met (*anticipated pain*) due to the status quo. Thus, pain occurs when people are paying the price for participating in a **dangerous** situation or are missing a key **opportunity**.

The accompanying illustration describes the relationships between current and anticipated pain, dangers and opportunities.

People generally are very frightened of the transition state and will try to avoid change where possible. A person will change only

	DANGER	**OPPORTUNITY**
CURRENT PAIN	**Situation:** Enrollment levels are down. **Pain:** Increasing budget deficits.	**Situation:** We can institute a revitalized student recruitment program now. **Pain:** Failure to improve the quality and mix of student body.
ANTICIPATED PAIN	**Situation:** We will suffer enrollment declines if we don't do "something." **Pain:** Expected erosion of market position.	**Situation:** We have an opportunity in the future to strengthen overall quality of our academic programs. **Pain:** Lose market position to our competitors.

©1989 by ODR, Inc., *Managing Organizational Change: Implementation Planning Procedure.*

when enough pain—present or anticipated—exists. "Pain management" is the process of consciously surfacing and orchestrating certain information to cause just enough pain to justify a person breaking the status quo inertia and entering the transition state. The pain level is relative to two factors: *frame of reference* and *pain tolerance*. Each person's frame of reference will dictate the degree of the perceived pain. The individual's tolerance for pain will then determine the actual critical mass point necessary for movement to occur.

The following story told by Daryl Conner vividly illustrates how pain affects behavior:

> *Some time ago there was a disastrous fire on an offshore oil drilling platform in the North Sea. Many men were killed*

in the disaster. One of the few survivors was interviewed a couple of nights after the accident by Ted Koppel on Nightline. The man described being awakened in the middle of the night by the explosion and the alarms, of running from his quarters to the edge of the platform, of jumping into the sea below, and of his subsequent rescue.

Mr. Koppel knew, however, that there was more to this story than the man's simple re-telling was revealing, so he said, "Now, wait a minute. Let me get this straight. There was all manner of debris floating in the water. The water itself was covered with oil, and was on fire. And yet you awoke from a sound sleep, ran immediately to the edge of the platform, and without hesitation jumped 15 stories into the water without any sure knowledge that you would survive the jump or that you would be rescued if you did survive the jump." Mr. Koppel paused for dramatic effect before asking, "Why in the world would you do that?" The platform worker did not hesitate even a second: "Because if I did not jump, I was going to fry."

This story illustrates perfectly that the pain associated with making a change will not occur until the pain of maintaining the status quo is simply too great to bear. The platform worker undoubtedly knew the risks of making his jump. He knew that death was a distinct possibility. If he did not jump, however, he faced explosions and roaring flames all around him. When it became clear to him that the possibility of survival by jumping—however remote—was better than the certainty of death, he jumped.

The above story illustrates how one individual experienced enough physical pain to cause him to act in a way he would normally be incapable of achieving.

For organizations, pain is represented in several different ways. The five pressure points cited below are the primary factors that cause enough pain for organizations to change behavior.

- *Past*: An organization has a history of unresolved prob-

lems or unachieved opportunities, such as a continual string of annual budget deficits.
- *Future*: The organization soon will initiate a project that produces a significant shift, such as a new payroll system.
- *Ambiguity*: The external market is more turbulent or competitive, or the internal organizational climate is less stable than in the past, such as increasing competition for qualified students.
- *Cost*: Failing to achieve key strategic objectives has high costs. This may mean unsolved problems or unexploited opportunities, waste of time, money and people resources, low morale or threatened job security. People also may learn to ignore strategic directives, or lose confidence in leadership when senior officers cannot successfully fulfill the promise of their strategic announcements.
- *Risk:* The risk of failing to achieve key strategic objectives also is high. How strong is the commitment of *sponsors* who possess the power to legitimize change? How resistant to the change are the *targets* who must change the way they work? How consistent is the change with the existing culture? How skilled are the **change agents** in developing sophisticated implementation architecture to address the project's human aspects?

A key axiom of change management is that major change always generates resistance that will be paid either by preventing or minimizing it, or healing from it. One way or the other, you will pay.

In summary, change is inevitable and essential to the survival of colleges and universities. Successfully managing change requires us to recognize change as a continual process rather than a singular event. The process of change entails three steps: the present state, the transition state and the desired state. Management focus must lie on the transition state since this is when change—and the most learning to adapt—occurs.

An organization can experience change in two ways, with distinctions of time and cost. The architectural approach requires careful planning, high upfront costs and considerable time to implement. The hammer approach uses force as its primary tool: The upfront costs are limited but the costs of maintenance are high.

Change will not occur without pain. The art of managing change is really the art of managing pain and its consequences.

3
Examining the Roles of Those Affected by Change
By Alceste Pappas

Managing change in higher education institutions involves interaction among many people playing different roles in the change process. Understanding the human dynamics is a key to success—and a common pitfall among institutions that have managed change unsuccessfully.

Why do so many planned changes in higher education fail? Do colleges and universities have a trait that creates this common outcome of change initiatives, or is the failure to implement change a pervasive management problem? Daryl Conner believes this problem characterizes most organizations today:

> *The major problem is not resistance to change, but the inability of managers responsible for the change to anticipate resistance, understand its dynamics and respond effectively. For example, most managers tend to become overly involved in technical components of a change project and neglect the human aspects. Managers often are unaware of the psychological phases people must go through to adapt successfully to changes affect-*

ing their work patterns. When these phases are ignored or not taken seriously, resistance to change usually increases. *

When the leaders of higher education institutions decide to solve a problem or pursue an opportunity that emerges with changing market conditions, they must answer a series of fundamental questions that may change the institution's strategy or culture. The leaders must anticipate how their decisions will affect others, and respond to resistance that inevitably will follow. They also must understand the critical roles of everyone affected by the change. An institution that wants to change its enrollment management process, for example, needs to understand how the change will affect each individual throughout the organization.

- *How will the proposed change impact the institution's constituency?* This may include the board of trustees, president, senior managers, administrative and support staff, faculty, students, alumni or legislators.
- *Will the proposed change modify the way the institution conducts "business?"* Will methods of decision-making change? Will committee structures that govern academic issues be altered? Will deans and directors, for example, have different responsibilities for recruiting new students? Will the financial aid office expect to have a greater role in the recruitment strategies?
- *How will the proposed change affect the "education product?"* For example, will new minority recruitment efforts mean a different student and alumni body in the coming years? If so, should the institution offer new academic programs and support services that serve the new "consumers"/students? How will this change impact student placement and counseling activities?

---

* ©1989 by ODR, Inc., *Managing Organizational Change: Dangers and Opportunities.*

Using the MOC terminology described in this monograph, organizational change involves the interaction of individuals identified as *sponsors, agents, targets* and *advocates.**

- *Sponsors* have the political, economical and logistical power to legitimize the change.
- *Agents* are responsible for implementing the change, as directed by the sponsors.
- *Targets*, the focus of the change initiative, are the ones who must change.
- *Advocates* are proponents of change. They do not have the power to sponsor the change or implement it, but can play an active part in helping promote the need for change.

Change managers must understand not only the roles people play in the change process, but also how organizational structures impact the relationships of those involved, and ultimately, the success of the project.

Critical Roles: Three Basic Models

First, let's examine how sponsors, agents and targets relate to each other. The basic models are discussed in order from the simplest structure to the most complex. The likelihood for successful change decreases as the relationships become more complex.

- The *linear model* has a direct chain of command within a hierarchial relationship. In this situation, the target reports directly to the agent, who reports directly to the sponsor. The sponsor has direct organizational power over the agent, who holds the same power over the target. Reporting relationships are usually clear and easily understood. Successful change is likely if sponsorship is

---

* ©1989 by ODR, Inc., *Managing Organizational Change: Implementation Planning Procedure.*

strong and consistent, the change agent is skilled, and the target is qualified and willing.

Using the example of change in enrollment management, the president would act as sponsor, the chief academic officer would be the agent, and the vice president of student affairs would be the target. In simplistic terms, the president may direct the provost to establish a comprehensive student recruitment program requiring the consolidation and reorganization of the admissions, counseling, public relations and financial aid offices. The provost, as the agent, would be responsible for directing and influencing the vice president of student affairs to reorganize the separate offices into one consolidated operation. (Of course, every individual in the offices affected also are targets of the change.)

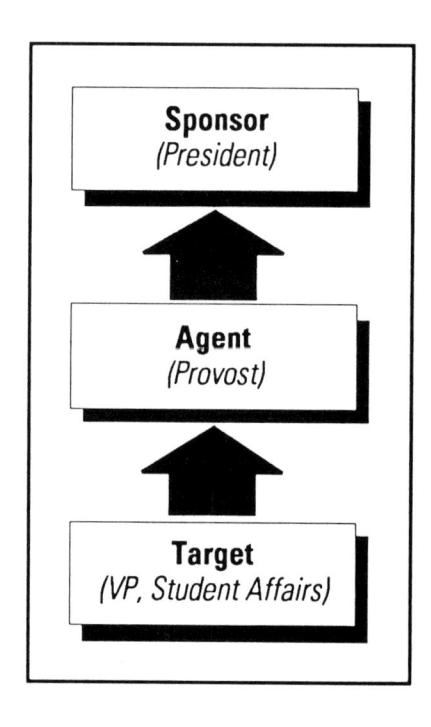

EXAMINING THE ROLES OF THOSE AFFECTED BY CHANGE 29

- The *triangular model* exists when the agent has no direct reporting relationship with the sponsor, but has been assigned the responsibility to implement a change that affects targets who do report directly to the sponsor. The reporting relationship between the agent and sponsor may be contractual, as in the case of an external consultant. The agent has no direct control or authority over the targets.

In this model, the agent's authority for changing the behavior of the targets comes solely from the sponsor's overt, continual and visible support. The targets will not listen to the agent if they perceive he (or she) does not have the sponsor's strong support.

In our enrollment example, the triangular model exists when both the provost and vice president for student affairs report to the president. In this model, the president, as sponsor, would assign the provost, as agent, the responsibility to change the behavior of the target—the vice president for student affairs. Since the provost, in this case, has no direct authority over the vice president, the provost's job as agent becomes more difficult and requires more direct, active support of the sponsoring president. Research conducted by ODR has shown that the triangular model of change fails 80 percent of the time.

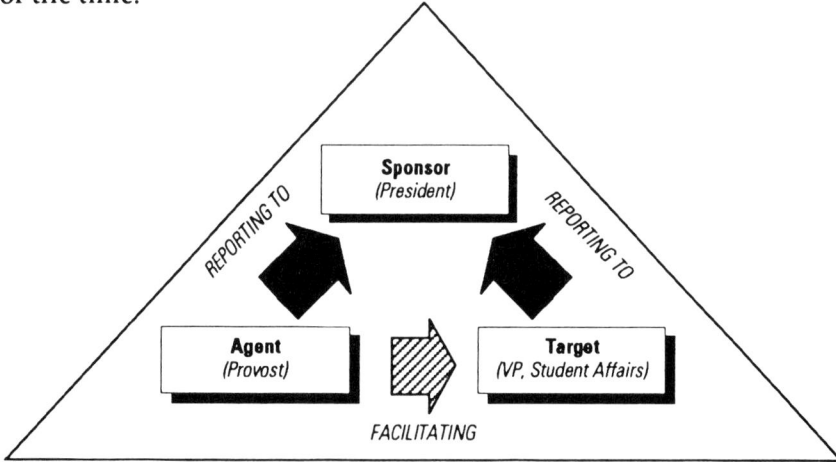

- The *square model* exists when the Agent reports directly to the sponsor, but the target reports to someone else in the organization. Change will always fail in this situation if the targets perceive that the initiating sponsor and agent have no authority over them to change their behavior. The square model is effective only when the target's superior is an advocate or supporter of the change.

In our enrollment example, the square model would exist when the provost is viewed as the initiating sponsor, who assigns someone on staff to act as agent to consolidate the offices of admissions, counseling, financial aid and public affairs—which are under the direct authority of the vice president of student affairs. This model will not work unless the vice president is viewed as an active, visible supporter of the change. This model has the most complex reporting relationships and requires the greatest skill levels and commitments of the sponsor, agents and targets.

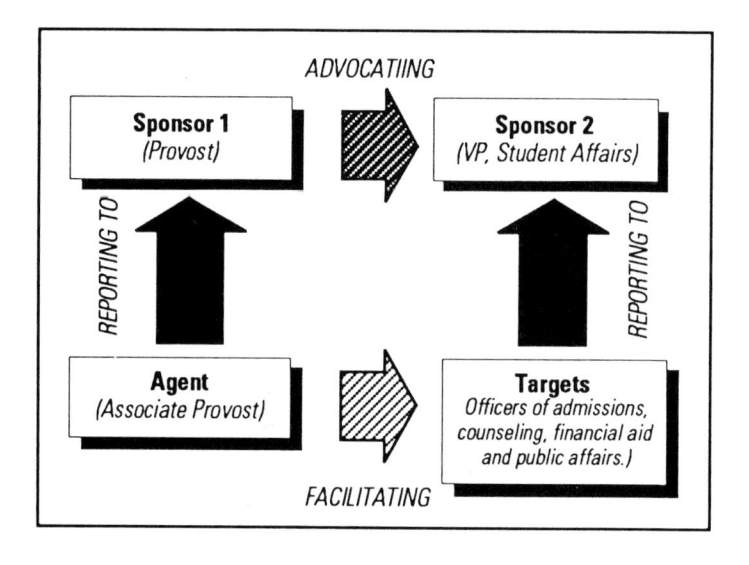

Critical Roles: Synergistic Relationships

The capacity of sponsors, agents, targets and advocates to work together as a team is determined by their working relationships which can be defined in three basic ways: ***destructive, static*** or ***synergistic.***

- A *destructive* relationship exists when individuals consume more resources—people, finances, physical space, etc.—than they create. They often are competitors. For example, when the admissions and financial aid offices do not cooperate, they become counterproductive and miss enrollment opportunities. A destructive relationship can be mathematically represented as $1+1< 2$.
- A *static* working relationship occurs when people interact in such a way that they consume resources at about the same rate they contribute back to the organization. In mathematical terms, the relationship is expressed as $1+1=2$. On the surface, nothing appears wrong with this relationship. But in reality it only works in a stable environment and is ineffective when change is necessary. For example, when the admissions and financial aid offices do not work together, they may meet their individual goals but do not support each other's programs, so they do not achieve optimal effectiveness.
- A *synergistic* working relationship exists when individuals work together to accomplish more than if they worked independently. Two prerequisites must exist for synergy to develop among sponsors, agents, targets and advocates. First, the team must share common goals and interdependence, or what Daryl Conner refers to as a "superordinate goal." The team also must believe this goal can be achieved only when all team members work together. This relationship is represented by $1+1>2$.

Four Phases of Synergistic Relationships*

Synergistic relationships are generated through a developmental process consisting of four interdependent, sequential phases: *interacting, appreciative understanding, integrating* and *implementing:*

- *Interacting:* The most basic condition necessary for synergy to exist within a working relationship is that the implementation team must interact. This phase provides the necessary conditions to allow team members to establish common change goals, acknowledge their independence and communicate effectively.
- *Appreciative Understanding:* Participants in a synergistic team must value and utilize the diversity that exists among the members. This phase develops a facilitating climate in which negative judgments are delayed, active empathy is demonstrated, and divergent perspectives are legitimized and valued.
- *Integration:* Synergy is the result of communicating, valuing and merging separate, diverse views. This phase brings individuals' views into a common perspective that can be supported unanimously.
- *Implementation:* The bottom line for synergy must be the successful implementation of important organizational changes. This final phase establishes the vehicle for the completion of the earlier stages. Previously developed synergistic energy is channeled into goal-directed, measurable action plans.

Managing change in college and university settings requires an understanding of the roles of each individual during the change process. Identifying who are the sponsors, agents, targets and advocates will aid in analyzing how each will be affected by the change,

---

* Based on ©1983 by ODR, Inc., *Building Synergistic Work Teams To Cope With Organizational Change.*

and what actions are necessary to move them through the change process.

Effective change management requires those affected by the change to work as a team, synergistically. Developing synergistic work teams is one of the most important tasks of effective change management. In fact, it would not be too much to say that synergy is the "soul" of successful change implementation projects, and if synergy does not exist, a change project will likely not meet its strategic goals. The good news is, however, that synergistic work teams can be built from non-synergistic environments. It requires a change in habits and patterns of thinking, but it is possible.

The model for synergistic work teams presented here can serve as an outline for identifying current behavior and its consistency with the kind of behavior needed for implementation success.

4
The Role and Responsibility of the Sponsor
By Brian Gorman

A sponsor is an individual who legitimizes changes within the organization. While advocates may encourage change and change agents work to help implement it, only sponsors are in positions of authority, holding the organizational power and influence necessary to legitimize a change project. Thus, sponsorship is a critical component in the change process.

The challenges of sponsorship in higher education are great because of the special organizational perspectives of faculty, administrators and the governing board. Faculty members' primary allegiances most often are to their respective academic disciplines, while administrators and boards are dedicated to the institution. A departmental chair may be the sponsor of change that affects curriculum requirements and the granting of tenure. The traditional autonomy of individual academic departments and even campuses in the academic systems makes the identification of effective change sponsors especially difficult.

Who is—Or Can Be—a Sponsor?

The key to identifying potential sponsors in an academic institution is to determine who holds recognized positions of authority and can exercise consequence control over targets —the individuals whose behavior you want to change. In the classroom, for example, faculty members are sponsors for their student's education. They are recognized authorities and control student consequences such as grades and determination of degree requirements.

In this example, identifying sponsors is relatively simple and involves only minor, direct and formal changes. The consequences of implementing the change—or failing to do so—most often would not be unexpected. The changes sought are insignificant from an organizational perspective.

How do you sponsor, however, a major change that will significantly impact your institution? Whose sponsorship is required to restructure how colleges and departments are organized? What if you seek to reaffirm a commitment to liberal arts, or improve the quality of undergraduate education? Perhaps those who attend your institution are considered "just students," and interest is growing to treat them as "consumers" or "customers." Who is in a position to control the consequences of everyone who must support the change?

In these cases, the identification of necessary sponsors is neither apparent nor direct. To properly identify them, you must understand how sponsorship works.

How Does Sponsorship Work?

In any change process, there is an *initiating sponsor* who legitimizes the proposed changes. The person must be in a position of authority and can exercise consequence control. The initiating sponsor must:

- Make strategic decisions regarding the desired changes.
- Issue senior-level directives regarding how to implement those strategic decisions.

- Take the necessary management actions to successfully complete these decisions.

Through this sequence, the initiating sponsor seeks to generate actions by others to implement the desired changes.

Within higher education, initiating sponsors of significant change might include the president, the vice president of academic affairs, the provost and academic deans. Occasionally, major changes are directly initiated in units that support the institution's educational mission, such as finance and administration, student affairs and institutional advancement. These support departments frequently advocate change.

Along with an initiating sponsor, successful change usually requires *sustaining sponsors*. The institution's officers can make strategic decisions and issue senior level directives, but they do not directly exercise control over all individuals whose support is critical to success. Thus, sponsorship must *cascade down* to sustaining sponsors who do exercise such control.

The task of identifying the appropriate sustaining sponsors is especially challenging in higher education. In most cases, the sustaining sponsors will include individuals within the formal organizational hierarchy—academic department chairs, administrative department directors, and so forth. Depending on the changes you seek and your institution's culture, sustaining sponsors also may include members of the faculty governance structure, union leadership, key student leaders, community leaders, board members or even high school guidance counselors.

Successful development of sustaining sponsors will lead to accurate, supported and durable change. These sponsors can interpret visible results and reinforce the implemented changes. On the other hand, not identifying the required sustaining sponsors—or failure to gain their support—will just as surely lead to unsuccessful implementation.

Challenges of Sponsorship

Significant changes call for difficult decisions. When those changes address issues of institutional mission, major organizational restructuring or other consequential resource allocations, the initiating sponsor must ensure there is sponsorship above—*endorsing sponsorship*—as well as below. Endorsing sponsors—typically a board of directors—sit above the initiating sponsor and may be called upon to show evident support for a change. We have witnessed situations where senior officers have sought to initiate such changes with apparently strong board support. Yet when the time arrived for making hard choices, board members revealed themselves as advocates, rather than sponsors. They still espoused support for the changes, but failed to take actions necessary to legitimize those changes.

An excellent example of how sponsorship was reaffirmed positively occurred recently in a project to integrate 28 VAX minicomputers at the Maryland State Universities and Colleges (MSUC). The project threatened to stall due to resistance from the target population—users in eight institutions throughout the state. The project managers knew they were in trouble if they could not get a renewed statement of sponsorship. So MSUC asked a consultant to review the original plan. The consultant recommended that the board of trustees reaffirm the original strategy for a centralized, coordinated network. The consultant also detailed a series of steps to allay end users' concerns. The original plan and the new recommendations were quickly and publicly approved by the organization's council of presidents and the board of trustees. This combination of substantive and ceremonial actions lowered target resistance, reaffirmed initiating sponsor support for the project, and brought on board sustaining sponsors who now knew they had the backing to drive the change throughout the organization.

As discussed earlier, the initiating sponsor's inability to control consequences for everyone who must support the change creates the need for sustaining sponsorship. Without sustaining sponsorship, the initiating sponsor will likely encounter the **black hole**. Astrophysicists tell us that the black hole is that space where energy becomes lost or seriously distorted. Or, as Daryl Conner says, *"Black holes are places in the organization universe where change directives go in but are never heard from again."* The outcome is the absence of change, superficial or short-term change, or other unintended results.

An initiating sponsor who discovers a black hole in the organization has three options:

- Use education and consequence management to help those who exhibit poor sustaining sponsorship see that such behavior is not in the organization's or their best interests.
- Replace uncommitted managers with those who support the change effort.
- Prepare to fail to achieve the stated change objectives.

What dynamics contribute to the "black hole" of academia? Ideally, in most higher learning institutions, the board of trustees or regents make strategic decisions along with the president or chancellor. The initiating and sustaining sponsors then articulate senior-level directives to vice presidents who subsequently work with deans and directors to take action and create change. These management actions yield visible results that are subject to all sorts of cultural interpretations by constituents. The ultimate outcome: participants either reinforce the intended result or generate new unintended results.

The following graphic illustrates the various scenarios contributing to the black hole. The vertical arrows depict strong circuitry that maintain and reinforce the integrity of the original intent. The striped arrows appearing at angles indicate weak circuitry that distorts the final consequences.

The sponsor plays a critical role in unfreezing targets' behaviors. During this early phase of change, people are motivated to discontinue or alter an aspect of behavior. The sponsor must understand what behaviors should change and devise a plan to accomplish the new, desired behavior. Only then can the sponsor routinely control consequences that foster the desired changes.

BEST CASE SEQUENCE	POSSIBLE	WORST CASE SEQUENCE
Decisions ↓	Decisions ↓	Decisions ⇝
Directives ↓	Directives ↓	Directives ⇝
Actions ↓	Actions ⇝	Actions ⇝
Visible Results ↓	Visible Results ⇝	Visible Results ⇝
Cultural Interpretation	Cultural Interpretation	Cultural Interpretation

© 1989 by ODR, Inc., *Managing Organizational Change: Implementation Planning Procedure*.

How to Achieve Commitment

Both initiating and sustaining sponsors face additional challenges as they develop the targets' commitment to change.

> *A person is said to be committed to a specific outcome when that goal is pursued in a consistent fashion. With the passing of time and in varying situations, the committed person persists in activities that, from his/her point of view, will help achieve the desired goal. The committed person will reject courses of action that may have short-term benefits if they are not consistent with a strategy for overall goal achievement. Finally, the committed person understands that a price will be paid. The greater commitment to a project, the more resources, like time, money, endurance, or self-control, and ingenuity a person freely invests in achieving the desired outcome... (Commitment) is the cement that provides the critical adhesion between people and the change goals.**

Achieving commitment to organizational change is an eight-stage process *(see illustration)*. The first is **contact**—the sponsor announces the planned change to the target. The initiating sponsor should discuss the proposed change directly with a future sustaining sponsor, rather than relying on media or another third party.

Contact does not necessarily lead to awareness. At stage two, an ***awareness of change*** emerges—the target becomes conscious of the planned changes.

In stage three, the target will develop an ***understanding of the nature and intent of the change.*** Prior to this point, the target was only limitedly exposed and lacked understanding of the information. The individual now begins to think in certain ways about the change. This stage is where resistance may first be apparent. The

---

* © 1989 by ODR, Inc., *Building Commitment to Organizational Change.*

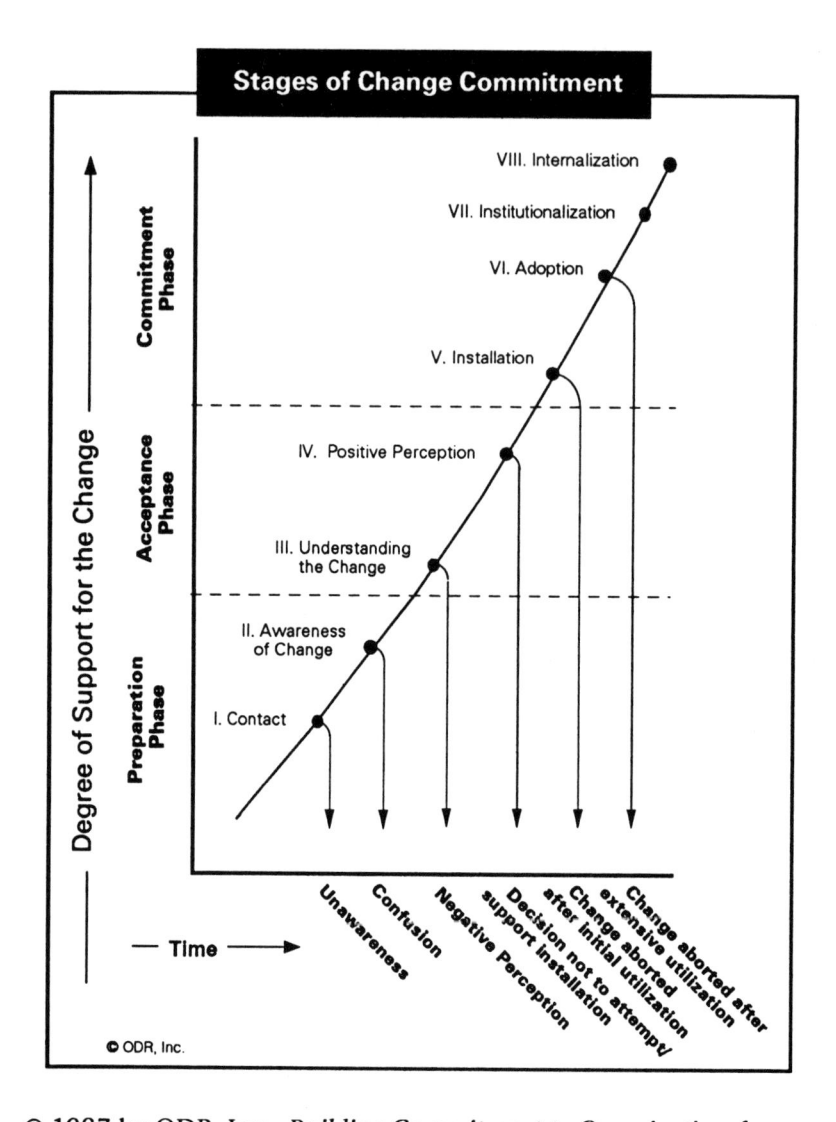

Stages of Change Commitment

- VIII. Internalization
- VII. Institutionalization
- VI. Adoption
- V. Installation
- IV. Positive Perception
- III. Understanding the Change
- II. Awareness of Change
- I. Contact

Commitment Phase / Acceptance Phase / Preparation Phase

Degree of Support for the Change → Time →

Outcomes: Unawareness, Confusion, Negative Perception, Decision not to attempt/support installation, Change aborted after initial utilization, Change aborted after extensive utilization

© ODR, Inc.

© 1987 by ODR, Inc., *Building Commitment to Organizational Change*.

sponsor must be prepared to recognize—and appropriately respond to—such resistance.

How strongly this resistance will emerge depends on how much the individual negatively perceives the change during the preparation phase. Sponsors should consciously build awareness and help individuals understand the change so they will perceive it positively. This is not always possible. An administrative restructuring that eliminates some long-held positions—or a redefinition of an organizational mission that phases out departments and programs—will not be uniformly accepted, no matter how it is presented. Thus, in planning for change, sponsors must recognize that targets may lack commitment—or even show conscious resistance—to the proposed change. This reality reinforces the need for sponsorship at all levels within the institution.

Stage four is where the target develops a *positive perception* toward the change. Without this perception, the individual will not commit the time, energy and other resources required to successfully implement it. Even with a positive perception, the target may determine that the required commitment is too extreme. Perhaps the risk of failure is seen as too great or the cost of supporting the change appears to outweigh the benefits.

The decision to implement the proposed change will require both positive perception and commitment. Sponsors must utilize their positions to legitimize the change with targets, and to assure that it will occur. At this point, the commitment phase of the change process begins.

Stage five is the *installation* of change—the first point for true committed action. Commitment is demonstrated through the investment of resources and consistent actions toward the fulfillment of long-term goals. Many people are willing to move to this stage because they perceive that even at this level of commitment the change is still reversible. In fact, many sponsors use reversibility as a strategy for getting targets of change to this commitment level. *"Let's just try the new software. If we don't like it, we can send it back."*

As installation occurs, it is almost inevitable that some unanticipated outcomes of the change will be identified. Perhaps future curricular changes make it difficult to recruit students for programs to be phased out. Alumni may become more vocal than expected in resisting proposed changes, and may influence institutional decisions through their contributions, the selection of board members, or—at public institutions—even through the legislature.

Adoption is the sixth stage of commitment to change. As in the earlier installation phase, the organization tests the change's cost and benefits, addressing logistical, economic and political issues. The proposed change is continually analyzed and modified, and even may be abandoned if problems are unresolved.

Although both installation and adoption offer reversibility, differences exist between installing and adopting change. While installation was concerned with starting the change, adoption's focus is longer term. Rather than addressing *"Can we do it?"* the focus becomes *"Do we want to continue it?"* Reasons to discontinue the change effort at this point might include:

- Logistic, political or economic problems arise that were not foreseen.
- The need that initiated an earlier commitment no longer exists.
- Changes in organizational strategic goals do not encompass the change outcomes.
- Key agents or sponsors leave their positions, lose credibility or ability to control consequences, or become less active in their support for the change.

Successful movement through the adoption phase leads to the **institutionalization** stage. The change has become a part of the organizational culture and is no longer viewed as experimental. At this point the need for formal sponsorship ends; the change is a part of the institution.

While institutionalization represents the highest degree of organizational commitment, it also presents some potential problems. Perhaps the most serious is when the targets have changed their behaviors, but not their beliefs. With less than whole-hearted support for the change, overall performance and effectiveness will diminish.

The next stage of commitment is *internalization.* At this stage, individuals become highly committed because they see change as congruent with their own interests, goals and value systems. The highest degree of commitment can develop only when people internalize change. Individuals act to satisfy their own needs, as well as the institution's. The targets of change become advocates or even sponsors, displaying enthusiasm, persistence and a high personal and professional investment.

These stages of change commitment, of course, are not always as clearly delineated in "real life" experiences. Individuals do not always move through these stages consistently, nor do the transitions from one stage to the next occur simultaneously for everyone. In some cases, the sustaining sponsors must go through several stages as targets before they can sponsor others. This adds yet another set of challenges to successful sponsorship.

Sponsorship means making difficult—and often politically unpopular—decisions. By its nature, sponsorship requires commitment and investment. Resources must be allocated differently and consequence control may result in alienating colleagues or subordinates. Traditions are challenged. Quite often, sponsors will find themselves opening and closing specific doors within the institution that others never knew existed.

One way to address these challenges is to involve targets when the change process begins. This may be difficult, particularly with organizational cultures that are clearly dictated by formal governance structures. Changes in tenure requirements, for example, cannot occur without the faculty senate's participation. The civil service committee will participate actively in changes to terms and conditions of employment. The student government association would exercise a clear voice on proposed changes for allocating student fees. Early and substantive involvement of targets in the change process is one of the primary ways to ensure a successful implementation project.

Characteristics of Effective Sponsorship

ODR's research on effective sponsorship has focused on identifying characteristics among managers of change that distinguish "winners" from "losers." Winners achieved the full human and technical value of their change decision on time and within budget, while losers either never accomplished their goals or did so after spending much more time or money than expected. Although strong sponsorship was by far the single most important difference between "winners" and "losers," very few managers fully understood the concepts of sponsorship. When asked to describe the sponsor role, most executives limited their comments to aspects of the process centered around making or announcing a decision. Most displayed a superficial understanding of the dynamics, and their performance for implementing change was low.

Those managers who were strong sponsors often relied on an "intuitive" sense. They accomplished their goals but could not explain how or why. We also found that executives who functioned effectively but without a conscious structure suffered from two problems. First, since they were not conscious of their sponsorship competencies, they erratically applied their intuitive skills. Secondly, because they could not articulate their actions, they did not translate their skills to others.

The following characteristics of effective sponsorship can help guide individuals who must lead the change effort: *

- ***Dissatisfaction with the present state.*** The pain of the status quo must be high enough to sustain sponsorship throughout the effort. The effective sponsor is consis-

---

* Based on: © 1989 by ODR, Inc. *How to be an Effective Sponsor of Major Organizational Change.*

tently aware that the organization cannot afford to fail at the change because the status quo is too costly.
- *Clear definition of the change.* The effective sponsor must clearly visualize the desired state. This vision ensures not only that the sponsor will lead in the proper direction, but also that resources are not wasted on efforts that do not drive the organization toward the desired state.
- *Strong belief that change should occur.* Major organizational change should be avoided unless the sponsor believes that the change will relieve the organization's pain. The sponsor should strongly believe in the need for the change, and be committed to the specific change as the right remedy for the problem. Otherwise, chances are the sponsor cannot fully implement the change.
- *Organizational impact of the change.* A change in one area often significantly impacts other areas. Effective sponsors understand how the proposed change will affect the complex web of relationships within the organization.
- *Human impact of the change.* In mechanistic terms, the small movements of big wheels at the top of the company often translate into frantic movements for smaller wheels down through the organization. The same is true of human systems. A major change that impacts only a single person is almost impossible to define, because any change affects not only the direct target, but also how the person relates to others. Effective sponsors of change understand how their decisions affect people and their workloads throughout the organization.
- *Amount of resources necessary for change.* Sponsors often underestimate the time, money and people resources required to implement change. This common mistake often results from not accurately assessing the commitments of the initiating and sustaining sponsors,

target resistance, the culture's ability to assimilate change, or the skill of change agents who build implementation plans.
- *Resource commitment.* Understanding the amount of resources necessary for change is essential, but effective sponsors also must be willing and able to commit those resources to the change project. Sponsors should realistically assess the competing demands on existing resources as well as future resource restrictions.
- *Demonstration of public commitment.* Sponsorship must cascade down through an organization, but the target audience must sense that top management legitimizes the change. Initiating and sustaining sponsors must manifest their commitment publicly so that the targets understand that their immediate sponsors do not act arbitrarily or without support from above.
- *Strong private support.* Skillful "behind the scenes" action communicates that the sponsor is not just paying lip service to the change project. The effective sponsor meets with key individuals or groups privately throughout the change process to assure continued support.
- *Consequence management.* A system of rewards and punishments should be used to sanction change. To accomplish strategic goals, a sponsor should measure and reward actions through consequence management.
- *Monitoring procedures.* Sponsors must periodically review progress toward the change objectives so that they can identify problems and take action to rectify the issue.
- *Commitment to sacrifice.* Major organizational change often requires that sponsors pay a personal and/or political price. The effective sponsor understands the real costs for success and leads the way in paying them, thus establishing a normative behavior that calls for sacrifice when the price of failure is prohibitive.
- *Sustained support.* The effective sponsor will do what it

takes for however long is necessary to successfully implement the change, and avoid consuming resources with short-term gains off the strategic path. Effective sponsors also understand that the organization should not undertake the change if it cannot afford to fail at the effort.

The above characteristics of successful sponsorship reinforce the need for systematic, committed and public support for the change, which will be witnessed throughout the organization by everyone affected by the change.

Opportunities of Sponsorship

The challenges of successful sponsorship are both tremendous and rewarding—particularly when the sponsors implement changes on time and within a budget. Experience has shown that success—when measured on the criteria of timeliness and budget limits—is all too rare. Because of their ability to control consequences for targets, sponsors play a critical role in that success.

Sponsors also have the opportunity to restructure organizations, bringing them into line with the organizational objectives. *"When you divide a whole into parts, it is the space between the parts which unites them."**   This same space can hold them apart. Successful sponsorship means changing how the parts of the institution are connected, perhaps in the formal reporting structure or in interactions between units. In either case, these organizational changes will support the broader changes in institutional strategy that are sought. A college's shift in its enrollment management procedures, for example, reflects responses to this opportunity.

The ability to architecturally change an institution's culture, discussed in Chapter 6, is one of the most exciting opportunities for the sponsor. Finally, sponsorship opens the door for personal and professional growth.

---

* Stanley M. Davis, *Future Perfect,* p.77.

Sponsorship Principles*

In this chapter, we have discussed the role of the sponsor in change. From this we can derive five principles of successful sponsorship.

- *Sponsorship is critical to successful change.* In the absence of clear and strong sponsorship, targets will perceive that the institution is not fully committed to the proposed change.
- *Weak sponsors must be educated or replaced, or failure is inevitable.* Only sponsors can exercise consequence control. They must fully understand the change's implications and take necessary actions to secure the critical resources. If they fail to fulfill the sponsorship role in exercising difficult decisions, then the change itself will fail.
- *Sponsorship cannot be delegated to agents.* While change agents can exercise certain responsibilities for implementing change, they are not in a position to legitimize it. Thus, sponsorship must be exercised directly by the sponsors.
- *"Initiating" and "sustaining" sponsors must never attempt to fulfill each others' roles.* While initiating sponsors have the authority to start the change process, they are too far removed from the full set of targets to sustain it. Sustaining sponsors have the necessary logistic, economic and political proximity to the targets.
- *Cascading sponsorship must be established and maintained.* Without sustaining sponsorship, change likely will enter the black hole. It may be temporary, become distorted or only superficially achieved. At each step of the cascading process, the targets must become

---

* Based on © 1989 by ODR, Inc., *How to Effectively Sponsor Major Organizational Change.*

committed sponsors for change and exercise their own consequence control.

Committed sponsorship is a necessary characteristic of successful change. Even when other important features of the change process are inadequate or not functioning, a strong sponsor can overcome adversity and resistance and accomplish the goals for change.

5
Understanding that Resistance to Change is Inevitable
By Warren Riley

Just as we recognize that change in our world is unavoidable, we must understand that resistance to change is also inevitable: Fundamental law of physics states that every action results in an equal and opposite reaction. This holds true for institutions where every major organizational change leads to resistance to that change.

Sponsors of change must understand several aspects of resistance before successfully implementing an architectural approach to change. They should know how frames of reference affect resistance, what circumstances cause it, how people express resistance and handle disruption, why they resist change, and how to manage reactions to organizational change for the best outcome.

Frames of Reference*

Frames of reference are those ideas, theories, beliefs, feelings, values and assumptions that allow each of us to apply meaning to our life experiences. In essence, frames of reference are the "glasses"

---

* Based on: © 1989 by ODR, Inc., *Managing Organizational Change: Implementation Planning Procedure.*

through which we see our world. They help us determine what is relevant or irrelevant, good or bad, a problem or opportunity, or an asset or liability.

Frames of reference are our guidance systems, helping us select behaviors for situations that happen to or around us. Our frames of reference—developed through our individual life experiences—determine what we perceive, think or expect, how we process information, what alternatives we see for making decisions and, ultimately, how we act. For change to occur in our institutions, targets must comprehend proposed change and respond based on their frames of reference. Two types of frames of reference exist: individual and institutional.

The MOC technology is based on the concept that an *individual* frame of reference is a set of values, range of emotions, knowledge base and behavioral patterns that we all develop and refine throughout our lives. Like fingerprints, each frame of reference is unique. For example, faculty members may resist an institution's plans to lower academic standards because they believe the change will diminish their prestige within the academic community.

An *institutional* frame of reference is based on the individual's position or role, understanding of and commitment to the organization. This frame of reference also encompasses institutional factors—logistics, economics and politics. These elements guide us in assessing change affecting the institution's strength, quality and viability. For example, we may resist our institution's decision to increase enrollments if we perceive that it will lower the standard of student admissions and depress the overall educational quality.

Together, the individual and institutional frames of reference form a guidance system for people as they face organizational change.

Disruption

The key to dealing with resistance is to understand that change equates to disruption. Without change, the environment is stable, predictable, calm and harmonious. With change, the environment is uncertain, unpredictable, stressful, dissonant, disturbed and upset. Three levels or degrees of disruption for individuals in the target group can be defined: no disruption, manageable disruption and unmanageable disruption.

An individual may feel *no disruption* when viewing the change through a frame of reference that determines the change is acceptable and easily accommodated. The change may require adjustments, but the target feels that adapting to the change will produce minimal problems. For example, a change in job responsibilities would cause no disruption if it does not materially impact status, substance or quality of the work effort.

An individual may feel *manageable* disruption when believing initially that the change will affect his or her equilibrium. In this case, the target's frame of reference fails to explain the change. This individual, for example, may be assigned increased duties but sees no promotion or salary increase.

A change manager can use three buffering systems to help the target understand and embrace the change. First, an *explanation mechanism* can help the individual understand otherwise unexplainable circumstances and provide a means for interpreting, anticipating and reacting to events: *"The increased work load is due to new regulatory requirements that affect the whole department."*

Secondly, an *anchoring mechanism* can remind the target of important organizational components—people, structure, policies, goals, rewards and leadership—that will not be altered by the change and will, as a result, provide targets with a sense of stability, continuity and identity: *"The increased work load will allow the department to meet its goals, and ultimately everyone in the department will be rewarded."*

Thirdly, *support/compensation mechanisms* are specific actions that ease or offset the target's discomfort experienced during traumatic change: *"In order to absorb the increased work load, temporary staff will be hired for two months to smooth the transition."*

These three buffering systems are important management tools for agents during the change process and are instrumental in achieving successful change when targets feel there is manageable disruption.

Finally, an individual may feel *unmanageable* disruption when the organizational change is so great that the frame of reference fails to support the proposed change and creates a situation of cognitive dissonance. The increased work load may be so heavy, for example, that stress results in the form of headaches, illness, despondency or irritability. In this case, the target sees the change as a crisis with unanticipated consequences and enormous uncertainty. The individual may become confused, counterproductive or dysfunctional. In this situation, the agent must develop the prospects for a favorable outcome by working—in an evolutionary or revolutionary way—to modify the target's frame of reference so that the change is viewed as less damaging or even positive.

An agent—and to a lesser degree, the sponsor—must try to predict the level of disruption that the proposed change will bring to the target group. The next step is to develop a plan that proposes a course of action to modify individual frames of reference.

Circumstances for Resistance

Targets develop resistance to change under a variety of circumstances: when they feel certain about negative consequences of change, when they doubt the positive consequences of change, or when they are frightened about the unknowns.

In the first case, a target reviews from his or her frame of reference the proposed change and concludes that negative consequences will occur, such as loss of job, power, influence, order, social environment, prestige or control. Even if the change has exciting, important positive significance, the target feels personally that the institution will experience clear and measurable negative consequences, and therefore will resist the change based on that assessment.

Secondly, a target may doubt that positive consequences will result from the proposed change or may not believe that the projected benefits of the change are legitimate or even possible: Can the efficiencies truly be gained? Can the relationships be established? Can the achievements be realized? The target, in this case, has reasons to believe that the desired positive results cannot be reached, and decides to resist the change.

The third circumstance—when the target faces too many unknowns about the change—is less quantifiable and more pervasive. While the other two cases included specific—though perhaps unfounded—beliefs about the results of the change, the third circumstance involves less concrete and more profound concerns. Most of us deal with unknowns throughout our lives. Our response to the ambiguity caused by not knowing what will happen ranges from mild concerns to profound anxiety. Each individual and institution has its own unique tolerance for ambiguity. When this tolerance is exceeded, resistance occurs.

Expressing Resistance

Individuals may resist change because they lack specific skills. For example, an employee who is not computer literate may resist the institution's conversion to a computer-based educational delivery system. Some may resist the launch of new fund-raising initiatives because they lack experience and do not possess the necessary skills to reach fund-raising goals. A faculty member may resist a mandate to perform research because he or she does not feel adept at securing sponsored funding.

On the other hand, an individual may resist change because of lack of motivation. In this case, the person possesses the skills, but sees no value in embracing change. This type of resistance can be more complex in nature and difficult to address because it is founded on an emotional response to the proposed change rather than externally verifiable data.

Resistance takes the form of either overt or covert individual behaviors or actions. *Overt* resistance is open, public and obvious. It may show up in a heated debate, when arguments against the change are articulated with vehemence. A member of the target group may resign or request transfer to another college or department, or a target may assemble a group of supporters and prepare position papers to fight the proposed change. In any case, this form of resistance is unhidden. If managed well, it can be a positive, constructive aspect of the implementation process.

Covert resistance is much less desirable in an institutional setting. This is a private, indirect, concealed or veiled response to proposed change. Covert in nature, it is destructive in intent to the proposed change and may take the form of sabotage. The target group's behavior may jeopardize some of the changes' underlying requirements. The root causes of covert resistance in an organization are a lack of synergy or no sense of common goals and interdependence.

In the case of a computer-based educational delivery system to be designed and implemented within the institution, covert resistance may lead to contaminating the date base through erroneous data input. In an institutional setting, covert resistance may consist of starting damaging rumors, handling job responsibilities with poor quality, slowing down or creating an unproductive work environment in the college or department. Of the two types of behavior and actions displayed by target groups, overt is more desirable than covert because the agent group can identify and address the problem. Sponsors and agents should, in fact, encourage overt resistance so that they can address and handle it.

Managing Reactions to Organizational Change*

Targets respond in predictable ways to change perceived as positive or negative. By understanding these reactions and applying certain tactics and techniques to manage the responses, sponsors and

---

* Based on: © 1989 by ODR, Inc., *Managing Organizational Change: Implementation Planning Procedure.*

agents can accommodate the concerns of targets and encourage successful change.

Even with positive change, targets respond with some pessimism over time *(see illustration)*.

The initial response to change perceived as positive is **uninformed optimism**: The target feels positive about the change and confidently embraces it *(such as a new promotion)*. Over time, as the target learns more about the change, a period of **informed pessimism** ensues: The target develops negative feelings and doubts his or her ability to handle the change *(first contentious staff meeting)*. Even with a positive change, the target may resist—overtly or covertly—by withdrawing from the change project. The target can potentially **check out** of the change environment *(cancel future staff meetings)*. If the agent senses a target is "checking out," the agent should develop tactics either to bring the target back "on board" or take him or her outside the bounds of the change project.

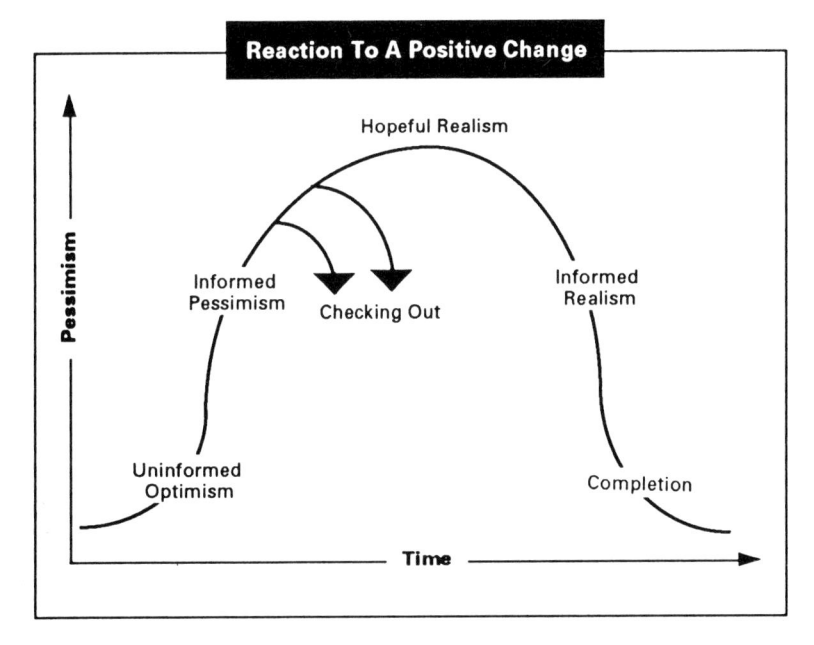

Reaction To A Positive Change

(Curve from Uninformed Optimism → Informed Pessimism → Hopeful Realism → Checking Out → Informed Realism → Completion; axes: Pessimism vs. Time)

© 1987 by ODR, Inc.

If the target decides not to "check out," the next step is ***hopeful realism***: The target perceives the change as achievable (*productive discussion with staff*). The individual feels less anxiety about the change and gains confidence to achieve the change results. Continuing the process, the target will next feel ***informed optimism***. High levels of positive energy and increased self-confidence occur (*take on new office project*) as success approaches. Finally, the target reaches ***completion***, strongly supporting the change (*becoming a productive manager*) and is even willing to assist others through the transition. These five stages, which describe the response to positive change, are part of all change projects.

The tactics of agents are critical to success in each stage. During ***uninformed optimism***, they should reinforce the targets' enthusiasm and prepare them for unforeseen difficulties. When ***informed pessimism*** occurs, agents should legitimize the negative feelings as a sign of learning, and provide encouragement and support. During ***hopeful realism***, agents should acknowledge how difficult the first accomplishments were and express confidence in the ability of the sponsor and target to cope with the remaining problems. During ***informed optimism***, agents should reinforce the change-related competence of the target and sponsor, and remind them that the follow-through is an important stage of the process. Finally, in ***completion***, agents should reward their achievements, help them identify important lessons and prepare them for the next task.

Just as there is a predictable response to positive change, a predictable response to change perceived as negative also exists (see illustration). In many ways it resembles the cycle of emotions that individuals feel when they experience the sudden death of a family member, a close relative or dear friend. The emotional response begins with stability and then moves to immobilization, denial, anger, bargaining, depression, testing and acceptance.

At the outset, the environment is stable: The target feels comfortable and in control. Then change—such as proposed staff reductions—is announced or diagnosed as necessary for the institution.

Response To A Negative Change

Figure: Emotional Response vs. Time curve showing Stability → Immobilization → Denial → Anger → Bargaining → Depression → Testing → Acceptance. (Based on work by Dr. Elizabeth Kubler-Ross)

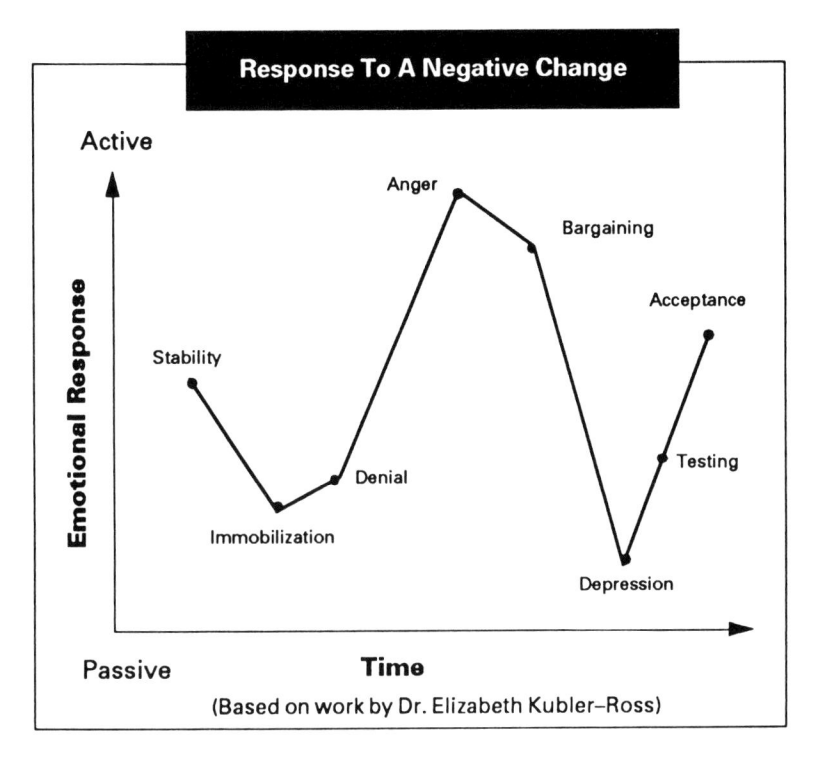

©1987 by ODR, Inc.

The target responds with fear, confusion and cognitive dissonance, feeling overwhelmed and immobilized. The target soon begins denying the possibility of the change—suggesting that it is an unacceptable reality—and behaves rather passively. Soon, however, the target becomes more emotional and angry, and tries to regain control of the situation—however unlikely or hopeless that might be. When the target senses futility, he or she begins to bargain with the sponsor, experiences a sense of loss and copes poorly. Once the individual realizes that change cannot be avoided or prevented, he or she tries new alternatives and new solutions. Finally, the target accepts the change and realistically responds to the mandate.

The tactics of agents are important during each stage. During *immobilization*, the agent should accommodate and accept the target's concerns. After suitable time, the agent should begin to do some reality testing with the target during the *denial* stage. When the target becomes *angry*, the agent should not take the attack personally and should legitimize the target's feeling by understanding that the reaction is consistent with the individual's frame of reference. During *bargaining* the agent should do further reality testing, this time in a more confrontational manner. As the target falls into *depression*, the agent should become supportive and encouraging. Next, the agent should help the target explore realistic options during the *testing* stage. Finally, as the target experiences *acceptance*, the agent should acknowledge the target's progress and plan for the future.

Perhaps the most important point to keep in mind is that a person's frame of reference largely determines whether a change is perceived as positive or negative. The successful change agent will manage information and consequences to make the change appear as the most positive of several possible alternatives.

Reasons for Resistance*

A number of barriers—some blatant, some subtle—can inhibit the successful execution of a change or quickly thwart even the most sincere efforts. A few common examples are:

- *Lack of vision*: When the corporate vision or specific business strategies are unclear, people may be confused about how to interpret the changes.
- *Poor implementation history*: When an organization has a history of poorly implemented strategic plans, members tend to expect little of substance when more new changes are announced.

---

* Based on: © 1988 by ODR, Inc., *Change Resistance Scale*.

- *Lack of middle management support*: Middle managers often lack any feeling of the ownership and involvement necessary for the enthusiastic support of change.
- *Lack of understanding or belief*: Managers and supervisors will not be effective change agents or supportive sponsors if they do not understand or believe in the change themselves.
- *Low risk taking*: A tendency to overly punish errors and reward the mere absence of mistakes promotes an environment of low-risk taking in which "nothing ventured, nothing gained" is more vice than virtue.
- *No consequence management*: When no positive or negative consequences exist for complying with a change objective, the targets of change will likely ignore any new directives.
- *Lack of clear communications*: If information about a change is allowed to filter down the organization in an unmanaged fashion, it becomes diffused or vague and is interpreted in arbitrary ways.
- *Failure to anticipate resistance*: All major changes, even those with positive implications, provoke resistance. People do not necessarily resist the change itself, but the disruptions it causes in their lives.
- *Poor management of resistance*: When resistance surfaces, it is often denied or suppressed. When overt resistance is not acknowledged and properly managed, it goes "underground," resulting in such covert activity as slowdowns, malicious compliance or even outright sabotage.
- *Lack of time*: If change managers allot too little time to implement change, they may experience huge maintenance costs. They must allow enough time for targets to internalize or subconsciously assimilate the principles of the change.

- *Poor follow through*: Many organizations launch major projects with great fanfare and reward those responsible for initiating the change, but then fail to follow through to see that the project achieves its stated goals.
- *Lack of synergy*: An organization's various operations—even widely dispersed components—are to some degree interdependent. If this fundamental point is overlooked, a change initiated in one area may encounter enormous resistance in others.
- *Rhetoric versus results*: Problems are sure to arise when senior managers say one thing about a change, but then behave in ways that send out opposite signals.

Easing the Resistance to Organizational Change

For most institutions, organizational change is conceived and managed in positive terms. Change is considered active, constructive and even creative in enhancing a college's or university's strength and stability. But while the subject is upbeat and exciting for most institutions, few plan for the negative aspect of change that is inevitable—resistance.

Specific management actions can aid you in securing organizational change:

- *Anticipate resistance*. Build its occurrence into the action plan to implement change. Take time to analyze the types of resistance that the organization will face. By anticipating resistance, you will not be surprised or stalled by it. Build steps into the timetable so that resistance does not destroy your schedule or jeopardize deadlines.
- *Think in terms of individual frames of reference*. Take as much time as required to examine the likely responses to the proposed change by every key target. You should know your target constituency well enough to think through their responses to previous experiences. Put

yourself in their shoes and generate a "mini" action plan for each target, knowing that each will respond differently.
- *Identify the conditions that underlie resistance and discuss them with the targets.* If you believe that target group members are convinced that the change will bring negative results, establish ways to review the benefits and support your position with similar examples. Similarly, if you believe target group members are uncertain about the positive consequences of the change, then develop information or contacts that help them see how the change was successful in another environment, or why the change is viewed as positive for the college or university. When targets are experiencing the fear of the unknown, provide more information that narrows the range of the outcomes and builds a base of understanding to support a carefully developed future for the organization. In each case, information is the key to unlocking the resistance to change.
- *Watch for expressions of resistance and discuss them with targets.* Where covert resistance is exhibited, engage freely in discussions about the change, its significance to the organization and the key role that the targets play in embracing the process. By creating opportunities for dialogue and discussion when first implementing change, agents can bring to the surface as many concerns as the targets wish to share, hopefully reducing the covert response. Much less difficult, but equally important, is the need to watch carefully for signs of resistance that appear unrelated to the change—those covert and insidious behaviors that will contaminate efforts to implement change. Where you believe covert resistance exists, you should communicate with the target and seek to bring the resistance to the surface, so that you can develop a workable solution.

- *Create a synergistic atmosphere.* The change process is most likely to succeed when the organization works synergistically. People are more powerful and capable of completing the change as a team than as a collection of individuals. Synergy draws out the team members' combined strengths and protects their weaknesses. Synergistic relationships among the team require a belief in a common goal—that the desired change is necessary—and an agreement that everyone must work together for successful change.
- *Understand the stages of commitment to change.* As discussed in Chapter 4, each stage of commitment to change must be reached in succession. Understanding these levels and developing programs to ensure their successful completion is critical. The sponsors and agents must be patient as they plan to implement change, recognizing that several stages are essential for gaining full and authentic support. From preparation and acceptance to commitment, the degree of support for change increases. Each juncture along the path can lead to positive or negative results. Agents must develop an approach for the activities and programs needed for a positive outcome at each juncture. A contingency plan must—like a safety net—catch targets who negatively respond to any step.

In summary, with the good comes the bad: Organizational change leads to resistance. As agents and sponsors, we must anticipate resistance and make it work for, not against, the institution. We must prepare for it and recognize its potential benefits. Resistance can build a stronger support for the change as members of the organization share information, communicate their concerns and analyze all aspects of the process.

6
Organizational Culture and Change
By Barbara Horst

> *Organizational cultures are created by leaders, and one of the most decisive functions of leadership may well be the creation, the management, and—if and when that may become necessary— the destruction of culture.*
>
> Edgar Schein, *Organizational Culture and Leadership*, 1985, p. 2.

Change managers must understand culture for one very simple reason: Whenever there is a discrepancy between the existing culture and a proposed change, culture always wins.

As a result, successful change sponsors and agents will modify either the change or the culture so that, in the long run, the organization possesses a strong culture that supports the changes that keep it healthy and competitive.

What is Culture?

During the summer of 1980, *Business Week* magazine ran a cover story about organizational culture. *Business Week* did not, however, invent the concept. Much has been written over the years about organizational culture, and it is a current topic of interest in many American business management writings.

Applied studies of organizational culture also proliferate. According to the American Anthropological Association, more than 100 anthropologists currently study U.S. corporate culture—a sure sign that American firms increasingly recognize organizational culture's importance to productivity and success.

Despite this flurry of interest in the subject, few managers seem to understand what organizational culture really is or how culture may affect proposed major changes. In some ways, culture can be viewed as an organization's self-concept. Analogous to an individual's personality, culture is complex and multi-dimensional. And like an individual's frame of reference, culture is a powerful guiding force for determining actions and attitudes.

What, exactly, is organizational culture? Daryl Conner defines culture as the *basic pattern of shared beliefs, behaviors and assumptions acquired over time by members of an organization*. Let's look briefly at the three principles underlying this definition:

Principle #1: Culture has *patterns* that can predict and guide appropriate behavior within an organization. For example, faculty at fictional Friendly College may have open-door policies regarding student office visits, while faculty at similarly fictional Regulation University limit student visits to posted office hours. Or, decisions at Friendly might be determined at any organizational level, while at Regulation only the president and cabinet make decisions.

Principle #2: Culture is *shared* by the organization's members, providing a cohesiveness throughout an organization, and enabling new members to quickly learn "how we do things around here." A new faculty member at Friendly, for example, soon understands that others expect her to be very accessible;

a new manager at Regulation quickly learns he must "feed" ideas to the cabinet.

Principle #3: Culture is *acquired* over time as a result of past successes. Friendly's open-door faculty culture may have developed first as a successful response to a previous retention problem. The strong central authority at Regulation may result from a response to an earlier financial crisis that required quick, centralized decisions.

Cultural patterns are built on shared *beliefs, behaviors* and *assumptions*:

- *Beliefs* are statements of what we hold to be true or false, relevant or irrelevant, good or bad, about our environment—such as Friendly's belief that accessibility is important.
- *Behaviors* are observable daily actions—someone who keeps regular office hours whenever they are not teaching, researching or attending meetings.
- *Assumptions* are unconscious rationale for applying certain beliefs or behaviors: Friendly faculty, for example, assume that high retention requires accessibility, though other factors may now have greater impact on student retention because of changing interests and needs.

These three building blocks describe two dimensions of culture: At one extreme is *conscious culture,* consisting of beliefs and behaviors that are intentional and overt—such as mission statements, goals and policies. On the other extreme is *unconscious culture,* based on assumptions that influence the organization unintentionally and indirectly—such as communications patterns, informal guidelines and "the way we do things around here." In between these two extremes exists a blend of conscious and unconscious beliefs, behaviors and assumptions that determine our attitudes and actions.

Culture can be a powerful tool to implement and reinforce

change, or it can impede the process. Particularly strong cultures with well developed patterns of beliefs, behaviors and assumptions may be very resistant to change, as are cultures that are largely unconscious.

How is Culture Formed?

Cultures develop in ways that are both unplanned and planned, through an "evolutionary" or "architectural" process.

The unplanned emergence of beliefs, behaviors and assumptions resulting from the organization's daily operations is *evolutionary* development. Such cultures result from a history of cumulative individual decisions. During the early part of this century, for example, faculty gradually obtained increased governance authority—particularly in matters concerning curriculum and selection of academic personnel. Over time, faculties have developed more *de facto* authority in these areas than governing boards, even though those boards retain legal responsibility for all institutional actions.

The proactive development and maintenance of beliefs, behaviors and assumptions is an *architectural* process. Such cultures result from strategic decisions about how an organization can meet certain goals. For example, in 1967 the American Association of University Professors published its *Joint Statement on Governance of Colleges and Universities*, which articulated the concept of shared governance and explicitly defined the faculty as primarily responsible for the curriculum, academic personnel decisions and the academic aspects of student life.

Evolutionary cultures often fail to support new strategic initiatives. Cultural patterns that served the institution well historically often are at odds with strategic directives that address a new environmental threat or opportunity. To make matters worse, managers often have trouble determining why people resist a new change, precisely because much of the culture is built on unstated, unconscious assumptions.

Let's take the admissions office as an example. During an expansion period in the 1950s and 1960s, most colleges had relatively small staffs and budgets for their admissions offices, whose roles were simply to review and respond to an increasing number of admission applications. But during the 1970s, the college marketplace changed drastically: the pool of prospective students diminished, and colleges required a more proactive admissions effort to remain competitive. Many colleges had trouble incorporating contemporary proactive marketing concepts within their old admissions cultures, because the new concepts required fundamentally different beliefs, behaviors and assumptions. Former admissions cultures, for example, believed that marketing is a private sector activity that addresses only sales and profits. Old admissions cultures had evolved over many years; new cultures had to be consciously developed.

In most organizations, culture is formed and reformed through an iterative process. Initial cultures are often developed architecturally by the organization's founders or original principal players. The culture then evolves slowly as it responds to various small changes in the internal or external environments. At some point, the culture may be consciously altered architecturally in response to a significant change.

How is Culture Conveyed?

Very few organizations can specifically define their cultures, although every organization has one. Describing an organization's culture is difficult because so much of it is unconscious. Although culture is sometimes difficult to describe, studies have shown that culture is conveyed through the following traits:

- *What are the leaders' real priorities?* Leaders' actions may be different from what they say is important. For example, your department head may request ideas from all staff levels, but act only on those from a few key directors.
- *How do leaders perceive and respond to crises?* Responses to campus racial tensions and unrest, for ex-

ample, may vary from "quick fixes," such as disciplinary actions, to longer-range responses that offer ongoing education programs or create organizations that bring racial elements together toward common goals.
- *What is the criteria for hiring, promotion and termination?* Again, actual practices may differ from written statements. A college may state that its faculty evaluation program gives equal weight to teaching and publication, but it may promote only those faculty who publish extensively.
- *How are power and status formally and informally defined?* In some institutions, academic department chairs are positions of power and prestige. In others, the chair is viewed as a chore that rotates periodically.
- *What is measured and controlled?* Are individual department budgets closely monitored, or is control responsibility broadly delegated throughout the institution?
- *What are the formal and informal policies, procedures and communications?* Who talks to whom? About what? How are decisions made? Who makes them?
- *What stories, legends, myths, rituals and symbols exist?* These can take many forms. For example, your college may hold informal sherry hours on Fridays for academic and non-academic employees. The president may routinely join students for luncheons. Or the memory of a particularly disliked autocrat may still influence how the faculty perceives administrators.
- *How are the physical facilities designed and used?* Do certain departments always receive better space? Are certain portions of the campus grounds better maintained than others? How does an office space and its furnishings indicate status?

By looking for these patterns of shared beliefs and behaviors, you can begin to uncover an organization's culture.

What is the Higher Education Culture?

The definition of culture is straightforward. The reality of culture in higher education is much more complex, because within most colleges and universities many different subcultures must work together synergistically to meet the institution's mission. How these subcultures interact, complement or collide determines the unique culture of each college or university.

Our *national higher education culture* exhibits characteristics that strongly influence most college or university subcultures. The national culture, for example, provides that lay boards of trustees govern institutions with a long-term perspective by holding institutional assets in trust for the public good. The temporal perspective of higher education is, in fact, long term: Decisions tend to be made slowly and fiscal policy is generally conservative. Change often occurs reactively rather than proactively. Access is important because education is viewed as both an intrinsically valuable process and a means for social mobility. Academic freedom is a cherished ideal, one that gives rise to the tenure system and significantly influences academic decision making and operations.

These cultural characteristics are further shaped and influenced by an institution's *"family" association*—whether it is a community or liberal arts college, a comprehensive or public university, or major research institution. The family association influences the school's curriculum, expression of access, approach to change, fiscal policies, faculty composition and governing structure.

Within the family, each institution has its own *individual institutional culture* that evolves from and reflects its unique mission, leadership, history, heritage, traditions, community and student profile. For religious, single-sex or minority institutions, the culture is further influenced by how the school identifies with particular social groups or causes.

Across these cultures lies the *culture of professionalism*. Teaching is viewed as a profession, as are the fields of medicine and law. The culture of educational professionalism possesses characteristics that are both common to all professions and unique to education. Faculty members place high value on intrinsic rewards, prefer to self govern and resist control by those outside the profession. They insist on academic freedom and autonomy, and value collegiality.

Academic disciplinary cultures are subcultures of professionalism. Faculty may insist on performance reviews by peers. They tend to recognize authority based on expertise rather than title and may be more loyal to their academic discipline than the institution. Each disciplinary culture also differs somewhat from all others. Cultural norms will vary among the humanities, social sciences, natural sciences and professions.

The governing board has another culture. Governing boards possess the ultimate legal and fiduciary responsibility for institutional strategies, policies and performance. Most boards are increasingly composed of business people whose cultural notions of organization, power and authority are notably different from those of faculty. Board members also tend to be more conservative politically and ideologically than faculty.

Finally there is the *administrative culture*, which is still very much in flux as college administration continues its transition from amateur to professional status. As the bridge between the trustees and the faculty, the administration often feels buffeted and misunderstood by both. And the cultural gap between faculty and administration is widening as institutions become more complex.

Management tools, modeled after those in private industry, offer more sophisticated approaches to the changing needs of institutions. As Robert Birnbaum has noted:

> *[Administrators] come to be seen by the faculty as ever more remote from the central academic concerns that define the institution. Faculty in turn come to be seen by the administration as*

> *self-interested, unconcerned with controlling costs, or unwilling to respond to legitimate requests for accountability.*
> (1988, *How Colleges Work*, p 7.)

As a change manager, you must ask yourself:

- Which cultures are influential on my campus, and which are not?
- Which are relevant to the change we are about to initiate?
- How strong or weak are they?
- Do the cultures operate synergistically or are they in conflict?
- Will the cultures support the proposed change, or must one or more of them be altered?

Remember: culture is so powerful that if a conflict exists between culture and a proposed change, culture will always win. The following section describes this potential clash between culture and change.

When is Culture an Issue?

Culture is always an issue when a strategic decision requires a major shift in how management and/or employees operate. Typical examples are:

- The adoption of new technologies.
- New management methods.
- Productivity improvements.
- Changes in senior level personnel.
- New strategies that require organizational subunits to work together more closely.

Culture is particularly important when an organization must redefine how to succeed in the future, as it reacts to a significant change in the marketplace or a major shift in how to serve the market. Recall the example of admissions offices that responded to a rapidly changing marketplace during the late 1970s. The Sputnik era provides another example: Overnight, scientific leadership became a key success criterion for America and its higher education system, requiring major changes in resource allocation decisions, prestige criteria and other cultural attributes.

Many large research universities are experiencing cultural shifts as they confront an environmental opportunity to work more closely with industry, particularly high technology firms. Universities have instituted industrial liaison and joint research programs, and are developing industrial research parks and consortia. Such ventures will speed the transfer of university research for commercial and public use, and can bring additional funds to the university through sponsored research or royalties for licenses of patented inventions.

As universities attempt to capitalize on these new opportunities, a culture clash emerges between the university's traditional emphasis on academic freedom and open inquiry, and industry's competitive need for secrecy in its research and development efforts. Another clash occurs within the university, which generally operates a slow, consensus-oriented, decision-making structure but now must respond more swiftly to the needs of its new industrial colleagues. Many universities are working through these cultural clashes because they view the new relationships as opportunities for financial and research success. The institutions have spent untold hours designing strategies to capitalize on the new opportunities, and they are changing the criteria of success for sponsoring research and generating revenue.

To ensure success, organizational operations and culture must be aligned with the newly formulated strategies to ensure success. The process of identifying the culture and its fit within the proposed change must be initiated by top management and orchestrated throughout the organization. Two key elements must exist:

- Develop clear statements of *vision: Where are we going?*; *mission: Why are we going there?*; and *strategy: How will we get there?*

- Analyze the consistency between the existing culture and what is needed to support the mission, vision and strategy.

What if the existing culture is inconsistent with the beliefs, behaviors and assumptions necessary for success? One of three actions will be required: The change must be redefined to fit the current culture, the culture must be altered, or both.

Changing Organizational Cultures

Because culture is so difficult to change, change sponsors and agents first should consider how to alter the proposed change. If this is not possible without threatening the organization's success, sponsors then must consider changing the culture itself.

But how does one alter culture? Cultural change requires extremely sophisticated change agents to guide a complex program of relentless rhetoric and communications, reinforced by specific, tangible consequence management. They should reward actions consistent with the desired culture and punish detrimental actions. Cultural change is an exceedingly complex, expensive and lengthy process that must be:

- *Initiated and legitimized from the top and given high priority and visibility.* Initiatives without top level sponsorship are generally viewed as "just another meaningless announcement."
- *Measurable, with meaningful and tangible objectives.* An audit of the current culture must measure specific beliefs, behaviors and assumptions against those desired within the new culture. Change agents should make specific comparisons periodically to verify actual progress.
- *Implemented throughout the organization, starting at the top and proceeding throughout each organizational level.* Sponsorship must directly cascade down from level to level and cannot be delegated to support staff.

- *Publicized in a gradual manner, primarily focusing on tangible results, not slick slogans.* Cultural management requires a lot of time and hard work. Change agents should wait to report a few concrete objectives when achieving them, rather than making dramatic promises that may take some time to keep.

Strong cultures found in higher education are typically difficult to modify: they require sophisticated plans with extended timelines to implement them. Change managers must understand the working relationships between key subcultures. For example, infighting among subcultures can disrupt efforts to change an organization's culture. Such relationships must improve and be more synergistic for the cultural change to succeed.

Summary

Higher education today faces both tremendous changes in its marketplace and opportunities to serve constituents in new ways. Demographic shifts, cost containment pressures, changing revenue structures, opportunities to work more closely with industry, rapid technological advances, increasing capital expenditure needs, and an increasingly interdependent and globally competitive economic environment represent some challenges and opportunities confronting today's colleges and universities. Higher education institutions must change strategically how they respond to these issues.

For changes to succeed, the academic culture must be aligned with the new strategies. Successful change managers must understand the various components of their institutional cultures and how these cultures will impact the proposed change. They also must know how culture is developed and conveyed, so that they can be proactive architects of culture. In short, successful educational leaders do more than manage personnel, finances, curricula, systems and services. They manage *culture*.

7
Taking a Structured and Disciplined Approach to Managing Change
By K. Scott Hughes

What makes a winner in managing a difficult organizational change? How do you ensure that a new compensation classification program will "work" or that a new accounting system will be implemented on time, within budget and to specification? What must the manager of a new high technology transfer program know to win? In its simplest form:

- **Winners** demand that the organization applies structure and discipline as it plans and executes all major changes.
- **Losers** apply the "spray and pray" approach when implementing change.

We all have seen "runaway" computer systems projects. What went wrong, and why were they out of control? Most often the organization lacked sufficient structure and discipline as it planned and executed the change. Decisions and actions either met uncontrolled resistance, were countercultural or had insufficient sponsorship.

This monograph describes change management concepts that emphasize the need to understand the change's impact on an organization and its people. These concepts also teach change managers how to anticipate and plan for the responses that surface during the change process.

The following case study illustrates many change management concepts described in this monograph. The example also shows how to manage significant organizational change effectively and avoid typical danger zones.

Case Study: Reorganizing Enrollment Management

In 1985, the trustees and president of fictional Alpha College became increasingly concerned about the college's enrollment trends. Alpha is a midwestern 1100-student independent, undergraduate liberal arts college that had experienced enrollment declines and lower SAT test scores by entering freshmen. The trustees and president knew that the demographic patterns would exert downward pressure on enrollments at least into the mid 1990s. The level of current and anticipated pain felt by both the president and trustees led them to become initiating sponsors of a new, comprehensive enrollment management program.

The board and president were highly concerned when they initiated this new effort because of several past attempts to implement major changes. Most recently, the college suffered through a disastrous computer system implementation that proved costly and demoralizing.

Led by a newly appointed board committee composed of members with extensive marketing experience, the college leadership consolidated major marketing-related activities and hired a new vice president of enrollment management who would oversee admissions, public relations, institutional research and financial aid. The committee had conducted a national search to find this experienced marketing-oriented admissions officer.

The new vice president was expected to be the sustaining sponsor and change agent responsible for restructuring the enrollment management functions and developing new marketing strategies that would substantially change old ways of thinking about admissions and recruitment. This individual also was expected to use the new board marketing committee as an advisory/approval body, and to show immediate improved results in the admission trends. As the primary change agent, he faced a Herculean set of tasks.

The board's marketing committee first asked the new vice president to prepare a comprehensive strategic marketing plan incorporating such new concepts as market analysis, promotional advertising campaigns, test marketing and targeted marketing strategies. Staff members of the newly constituted Enrollment Management Division were excited about their new responsibilities and had visions of expanded programs and new marketing initiatives. Their new marketing thrusts caused recruiting expenditures to increase by more than 40 percent in the 1987-88 fiscal year.

Not everybody was pleased with the new marketing concepts. Several key constituent groups who, if brought on board could have been valuable agents, strongly resisted changes that conflicted with many of the college's long-standing cultural norms. Many faculty were upset that increased resources were allocated for new marketing programs, and thought the more blatant type of college recruitment was distasteful and conflicted with the college's traditional conservative values. The faculty's unrest drew concern by the president and irritated the governing board.

Another constituency distressed by the new marketing initiatives was a group of loyal alumni who for many years had been a major volunteer resource in identifying and recruiting students in major metropolitan areas throughout the Midwest and East Coast. The alumni were not included in the new marketing program initiatives and felt slighted that their historic recruitment role was no longer considered relevant. They, too, frequently voiced displeasure to the president and the board.

By fall 1988, the new enrollment program was at a critical juncture:

- The new marketing program initiatives resulted in outstanding recruitment numbers for fall 1988—freshman enrollment rose by 17 percent and the SAT scores had stabilized.
- Admissions costs had risen by 40 percent, and an increase of 25 percent was expected for the 1988-89 fiscal year.
- The vice president had failed to present a cogent marketing plan to the board's marketing committee. With no clear set of objectives or strategies in place, the increased enrollments were considered simply a result of more effort rather than "smarter" effort.
- The faculty and alumni continued their vocal resistance about the need or propriety of the new marketing initiatives.
- The enrollment management staff, feeling pressure and criticism from the board, faculty and alumni, became disillusioned and frustrated because they did not receive the recognition they deserved for the increased enrollment levels.

At this point, the president lost confidence in his change agent, who in spite of successful quantitative results, failed to fully integrate the change into the college's culture and belief structures. The vice president resigned in late 1988.

What major danger areas jeopardized the change agent's success and cost him his job? Major factors to consider were:

- *Lack of effective pain management by the vice president.* The vice president did not adequately manage the expectations of the board or president.
- *Lack of a comprehensive change plan.* The vice president's new marketing initiatives did not fit within an overall strategic framework that sponsors and targets could understand.

- *Lack of a cultural understanding.* The vice president did not anticipate the jarring impact of his changes on the college's traditional cultural values and beliefs. He did not plan to use the culture or seek ways of changing the culture to accept his new programs.
- *Lack of resistance management.* The vice president failed to anticipate that faculty and alumni would resist the changes, nor did he recognize them as important targets in the change process. He made no effort to develop a frame of reference for the faculty and alumni, or to devise strategies to diffuse their resistance and ultimately change their behavior to accept the change.

After accepting the vice president's resignation, the president hired external consultants to evaluate the situation and to recommend how to follow through with fully implementing and integrating the enrollment management program. The subsequent efforts of the consultants, acting as change agents, led to actions that overcame the resistance first experienced by the sponsors and targets.

The college, over the next six months, took the following actions that led to successful changes:

- Developed a strategic marketing plan and budget and submitted the package for board approval in January 1989.
- Assigned the enrollment management function to the current vice president for student affairs. He became the change agent, understanding the cultural barriers and resistance of the faculty and alumni.
- Identified specific strategic options, each with resulting costs and potential benefits. These costs took into account both the human and the technical aspects of implementing the changes.
- Met with the alumni association, reinstituted the alumni recruitment program and added alumni representatives to the board marketing committee.

- Implemented a series of ongoing faculty meetings to describe how the new marketing program would impact the student mix, quality and curriculum. These meetings also allowed sponsors and agents to monitor resistance and make ongoing adjustments to the implementation plan.
- Initiated a campus visit recruitment program using faculty volunteers.
- Established an activity reporting system to document marketing activities and results, and reported frequently to the president and board marketing committee.

Interesting results followed: The college recruitment efforts for fall 1989 were again successful—up 15 percent. Faculty resistance continues, but because various feedback mechanisms are in place—including meetings and the use of survey instruments—the resistance is overt and has, in fact, become a positive force in the project. Ultimately the faculty perspectives may modify the board's more aggressive marketing thrusts. Some alumni volunteers remain disenchanted, but others have found new and exciting ways to support the recruitment efforts.

The board's marketing committee is extremely pleased with the results of its initiatives in spite of continued increases in marketing costs. Now the board can examine detailed budgets and performance indicators and evaluate the relative success of the different marketing strategies.

Sequence for the Implementation Planning Procedure

We began this chapter talking about winners. How do winners make change work? They demand that the organization applies structure and discipline as it plans and executes all major changes. Winners know where they stand throughout the entire change process, recognizing the primary factors for success and assessing the risk levels for each factor.

TAKING A STRUCTURED AND DISCIPLINED APPROACH

In our Alpha College case study, ultimate success resulted from a systematic approach that addressed each key resistance area raised by the targets and sponsors.

The following 12-step process defines the factors that contribute to successful change. The process draws on the concepts discussed throughout this monograph.

Implementation Planning Procedures

Step	Alpha College
1. Has the change been thoroughly defined?	The new marketing vice president did not take the board's advice to prepare a marketing plan. A first step in the revised effort was to develop a strategic marketing plan and budget. An initial implementation plan should also be developed at this time which takes into account sponsor committment, cultural readiness, target resistance, and the skill of the change agents. The lack of a comprehensive plan was a major reason for the initial failure.

The use of surveys and diagnostic instruments can help answer the following questions <u>before</u> implementation is attempted:

2. Will the change disrupt the organization?	The new marketing program affected the board, faculty, alumni, and the college's culture. The enrollment management program can affect all aspects of the college environment.
3. Is there a history of implementation problems?	The college has a history of inept change management and everyone hesitates to accept new challenges.

4. Is the disruptive change consistent with the existing culture?	The initial changes attempted in enrollment management—particularly recruitment—were countercultural. The new vice president had discounted how an active alumni and the use of low-key promotions had created an understated, conservative image.
5. Will sponsors scale back if the change is too countercultural?	The new program's countercultural aspects were greater than the president could sponsor. The leader backed off after receiving too much heat from the faculty and alumni.
6. Are the sponsors sufficiently committed to the change project?	The president and board marketing committee showed sufficient commitment to the new enrollment management program. Ultimately, they knew that Alpha College must be more competitive and overcame their short-term discomfort when first attempting the new vice president's insensitive approach.
7. Is the current organizational stress level too high?	The initial stress level was not too high. The enrollment management staff was excited about the new program and the college invested significant resources to achieve desired results. The stress level increased rapidly, however, when the vice president failed to properly manage the change.
8. Are the target groups prepared to work together to implement change?	The alumni and faculty were not asked to participate at first and their resistance level caused dysfunctional attitudes and actions. Ultimately, when the faculty and staff joined the process, they were ready to implement the change.

9. Is the target resistance low?	Again, the alumni and faculty may have started out with low resistance, but that quickly disappeared when they felt mistreated.
10. Are the change agents sufficiently skilled?	The new vice president had no concept of how to effectively manage the change process. He used the hammer approach and did not invest in healing the pain that he created. Ultimately, the vice president for student affairs was much more sensitive to each target group's frame of reference and built successful healing programs.
11. Do the sponsors, agents and targets work together synergistically?	The process started disastrously. The board marketing committee members quickly lost faith in the new vice president when they saw destructed relationships—an alienated faculty and alumni, a demoralized staff and a defensive president. The second phase was much more synergistic and productive. The separate groups began trusting each another, built strong communications channels and recognized the need for interdependence.
12. Does the overall assessment of the change factors described in the prior steps warrant a continued process for change?	If the president and board had addressed these issues as the project began, they would not have suffered the initial consequences. Ultimately, the consultants and student affairs vice president integrated the questions when they took over the change process and developed a new work plan.

The steps outlined above consolidate the major change management concepts described throughout the monograph. Change management is not haphazard or unplanned. It is a systematic understanding of how people react to change, and how to motivate them even when the change negatively affects them.